STEPDADS
SHOWING UP!
&
SHOWING OUT!

9/20/20

*To Devon Vincent Wayne White,
Thanks for the opportunity to learn "how to sing" in the choir. I have grown under your musical and spiritual leadership. God Bless!*

Sebahle Charles Rue SCR

STEPDADS

SHOWING UP!
&
SHOWING OUT!

Tips for Navigating the Complex
World of Blended Families

SEDERICK C. RICE, Ph.D

iUniverse

STEPDADS SHOWING UP! & SHOWING OUT!
TIPS FOR NAVIGATING THE COMPLEX
WORLD OF BLENDED FAMILIES

Copyright © 2020 Sederick C. Rice, Ph.D.

All rights reserved. No part of this book may be used or reproduced by any means, graphic, electronic, or mechanical, including photocopying, recording, taping or by any information storage retrieval system without the written permission of the author except in the case of brief quotations embodied in critical articles and reviews.

Scripture taken from the King James Version of the Bible.

iUniverse books may be ordered through booksellers or by contacting:

iUniverse
1663 Liberty Drive
Bloomington, IN 47403
www.iuniverse.com
844-349-9409

Because of the dynamic nature of the Internet, any web addresses or links contained in this book may have changed since publication and may no longer be valid. The views expressed in this work are solely those of the author and do not necessarily reflect the views of the publisher, and the publisher hereby disclaims any responsibility for them.

Any people depicted in stock imagery provided by Getty Images are models, and such images are being used for illustrative purposes only.
Certain stock imagery © Getty Images.

ISBN: 978-1-6632-0694-7 (sc)
ISBN: 978-1-6632-0695-4 (e)

Print information available on the last page.

iUniverse rev. date: 09/03/2020

CONTENTS

Dedication vii
Thank You Daddy! Miss You! Love You! ix
Foreword xi
Acknowledgements xv
Epigraph xvii
Preface xix
The Greatest Stepfather in History xxiii

Year 1 1
Year 2 23
Year 3 31
Year 4 41
Year 5 51
Year 6 67
Year 7 81
Year 8 143
Year 9 151
Year 10 155

Year Chapter References 160
Foreword Author 202
Proofreader/Editor 204
Author Biography 210

DEDICATION

DEDICATION

THANK YOU DADDY!
MISS YOU! LOVE YOU!

Father, Grandfather, "Big Brother Almighty," Uncle Charles, Wise Counselor, Veteran of a Foreign War (Navy), Leader, Friend, Principled, Kind, Disciplined, Square Dealing, Giving, Ethical, Moral, Chauffeur, Courier, Math Teacher, Educator, Auto Mechanic, Electrician, Plumber, Carpenter, Cook, Farmer, Avid Gardener, Antiques and Collectibles Dealer, Junk MAN, and Flea Market Legend (PINECREST and Hwy. 79 locations, Pine Bluff, Arkansas) **Charlie Rice!!!**

FOREWORD

The Cambridge Dictionary defines him as "the man who is married to someone's mother but who is not their real father." Dictionary.com defines him as "the husband of one's mother by a later marriage." Wikipedia defines him as "a non-biological male parent married to one's preexisting parent." He frequently has these definitions and other words and phrases hurled at him from countless directions and from multiple perspectives. He has been lifted as a hero and he has been scorned as a forced substitute by some and a pseudo-father-wannabe by others. He has been accepted when no one else would step up to the plate and he has been cast down as simply unwanted.

He is the step-father and he may be weary of these and other opinions that are passed his way but the engaged step-father is resolute in his disposition of duty regardless of what may attempt to impede his progress. His way may be blocked with walls built around some hearts, emotional pitfalls and traps laid by many, and insecurity and incompetence from what life has thrown at this patriarch without being given the chance by the family. However, his way can be paved with acceptance, love and understanding when given a chance. In the best and worst of family structures, the step-father is an individual that daily must utilize what Bolman and Deal reference as the 'four frames of leadership'; structural, human resources, political, and symbolic. Those frames must then be multiplied by love and patience while sometimes being divided by time and emotional block.

The structural frame of the step-father has him focused on getting the job of being a father accomplished. For the engaged step-father, there is no difference in being the biological father or the biological father's replacement. His aims are to cover his household with protection and providence. His daily plan focuses on how to achieve these outcomes. He is strategic in his actions, words, and emotions. Everything becomes a calculated chess-move with desired outcomes for every action. He thinks and rethinks what he does as if there is a matrix or rubric being used to calculate his every move. This makes him extremely procedural and detailed. Very often this is necessary because he really is being scored by those around him. The wife, children, and even extended family gauge his actions and continually score his activity and performance. For this reason, the family is frequently looked at by the step-father in terms of systems and processes that must be revised and repurposed for success. Fair or not, he continues to try to improve every family procedure, policy, and practice in order to increase efficiency and effectiveness. Most of his time is spent in this structural frame of mind.

The step-father oftentimes must become a specialist within the human resources frame. He is continually focused on the needs and wants of those around him. He is responsible for not only his well-being but that of the family as well. Quite frequently, he will put his own needs and wants behind those of the other family members as he lives as though he is the object of the statement between Captain Kirk and First Officer Spock in Star Trek: The Wrath of Khan, "the needs of the many outweigh the needs of the few or the one." His entire being is focused on fulfilling the family's needs for growth and development, uplifting their spirits, edifying their weaknesses, and building their happiness. The satisfaction of the family, from every aspect, becomes his daily task and burden. Most of the time, he becomes 'the one' cheerfully. The engaged step-father spends much of his emotional collateral and resources in the political frame of mind.

The step-father's political frame sees him continually looking for leverage, building alliances and hoping for allegiances with the family. He has to always be aware of ulterior motives and hidden or conflicting agendas from the family members with whom he seeks to unite and blend. This forces him to always be trying to get buy-in from family members and be ready to intervene with conflict-resolution tactics to hold the many family members together at all times and through all occurrences. Although he cannot run for the vacated position of father, he works for write-in votes tirelessly. In the political frame is where the engaged step-father spends most of his mental energy.

Lastly, the symbolic frame for the step-father has him always working to fill the role of father. He is the one responsible for protecting and providing, making family moments of laughter, being relied on for advice, information, insight, and love, the quintessential male presence, the family's Superman! He works without end to give the family every reason to believe in him and the idea of family that he tries to create for them. Everything that is wrapped up into the term 'father', the step-father tries to do sometimes with one arm, blindfolded, and starting a lap behind in the race to be the family's number 1!

In *StepDads, Showing Up! & Showing Out!* Dr. Sederick Charles Rice has wrapped all of these concepts, realities, theories, stories, and memoirs into one profound work. This work will be advice to some, giving them some information about the role in which they may find themselves. It may be encouragement to some, giving them some hope to believe in and showing them that they are not the only person to have been in this role. This book may be entertaining to some as it gives Dr. Rice's first-hand accounts of family situations which may make you laugh, cry, or sit back and contemplate on the many requirements and necessities of a step-father. Through it all, the value of this book, like the value of step-fathers universally, is priceless! Enjoy the read!

Showing up & Showing out,
Dr. Josiah J. Sampson, III

ACKNOWLEDGEMENTS

I first thank God for His many blessings, favor, correction, grace, mercy, and the ability to write this book. I also thank God for putting people in my life to help me to grow mentally, spiritually, physically, emotionally and financially. Thank You to my Wife, Mother-in-law, and the children for their love and support. Thanks to my close and extended family members from the Spears, Rice, Jones, Bohannon, and Seals families for their continued Love, Support, Guidance, and Patience. Thank You Uncle Kim for being a "soldier" for daddy (Big Brother Almighty), when he was in the hospital and making sure he received the best care. Thank You to the faculty, staff, students, and administrators at the University of Arkansas at Pine Bluff (UAPB) for the opportunity to train and work to make an impact at an Historically Black College and University (HBCU), and my Alma Mater. Thank You to the Center for the Advancement of STEM Leadership (CASL) Cohort II leadership, coaches, staff, and fellows for the wonderful professional leadership learning experiences, which have prepared me to "Lead with Soul" at HBCUs. Thank You Dr. Robert Carr for your leadership as Provost and Vice-Chancellor for Academic Affairs at UAPB, and for seeing my potential for future administrative opportunities. Special thanks to Dr. Josiah J. Sampson, III for the Foreword, CA DESIGNS Media & Design Studio for the book cover, Cary R. Clayton for the StepDaddy Photoshoot pictures, and David Maddox and Fathers and Sons Clothier for community presence and support. Thank You Dr. Reed for recommending Miss Betty S. Willingham to proofread and edit this book. Special thanks to my church family and The Daniels, Everetts, and Graves' families for your care and support. Thank You to the readers of this book. I hope this work sparks some thought, dialogue, laughter, and reflection in your own lives. I am too old for "Peer Pressure," so I had to be "Authentic." God Bless!

EPIGRAPH

"I AM A LEO"
August 8

Positive Traits	Negative Traits
Enthusiastic	Vain
Determined	Egotistical
Ambitious	Childish
Creative	Overbearing
Generous	Stubborn
Dynamic	Pretentious
Loyal	Fears Ridicule
Romantic	Bossy
Decisive	Dogmatic
Leader	Demanding
Humorous	Controlling
Protective	Needy

PREFACE

> GOD, GRANT ME THE **SERENITY** TO ACCEPT THE THINGS I CANNOT CHANGE, THE **COURAGE** TO CHANGE THE THINGS I CAN, AND THE **WISDOM** TO KNOW THE DIFFERENCE

(Serenity Prayer- Reinhold Niebuhr (1932-1933)

StepDads, Showing Up & Showing Out is a humorous and interesting view of my growth, development, perspectives, and experiences as a STEPFATHER (STEPDAD) over the last almost ten years. This book contains stories, learning curves, experiences, and opinions designed to give support, provide wisdom and encouragement to those MEN, (and the WOMEN who love and adore them), who have taken on the **Difficult, Stressful, Mind-Blowing, Frustrating, Awesome, Honorable, Humbling, Rewarding, Enriching,** and **Blessed** opportunity to be somebody's STEPFATHER (STEPDAD). Stepdads Showing Up & Showing Out will also be an inciteful reference for MEN (and the WOMEN who love and adore them) to help them understand and cope with some of the circumstances and situations that may arise in blended families. You have to laugh a lot to make it in a blended family. "Humor is still the best medicine."

Throughout this book, I will refer to myself as "**Mr. Sederick**," which will be explained in Year 1. I will also outline the type of support I need from my Wife, Mother-in-law, close friends, pastors, deacons, family members, The Bible, self-help books, webinars, seminars, vlogs, YouTube videos, PowerPoint Lectures, and prayer to deal with the pressure as a STEPFATHER (STEPDAD). I had to learn and understand the motivations of serious bodybuilders and professional athletes, who often rely on the famous phrase "**I Command You to Grow!**" which is related to the "Mind Over Matter Attitude" a person must have to achieve greatness in any area. This is the same mentality I had to develop to successfully operate in a STEPFATHER (STEPDAD) role. I had to grow in patience, self-reflection, understanding, wisdom, finances, and spirit.

Now, let us discuss Blended Families....

There are several types of blended marriages which often lead to blended families. The examples I highlight may or may not relate to your situation, but the knowledge is foundational to the theme of the book. In one blended family scenario, a man with children marries a never married woman with no children. A second blended family scenario can occur when a woman with children marries a man with no children. A third scenario could occur when a divorced mom, with children, marries a divorced man with children. This is the *Brady Bunch Model*, a popular television show that was broadcast in the late 1960's and into the early 1970's. A final blended family scenario could occur when a widow or widower with children remarries. This is the *Step Brothers' Model*, which was a 2008 movie starring Will Ferrell and John C. Reilly, which "highlighted the adventures of two aimless middle-aged losers still living at home and forced against their will to become roommates when their parents marry" (Ferrell, 2008). It is no coincidence that my blended family references relate to situation comedies and funny movies. To make it in a blended family, comedy and laughter are very important.

Many adults, including myself, were unprepared for blended family life. Adults in blended families often parent uncomfortable children, while stepparents usually bring new expectations, traditions, and habits, which can cause tension. Further, adults in blended families must often choose to support their children or spouses (Gillespie, 2018). There is a bright side! There are benefits to a blended family, including 1) Additional Parental Guidance, 2) Increased Financial

Support for the Family Unit, 3) Increased Emotional Support for Children and Spouses, 4) Increased Family Unit Stability, and an opportunity to 5) Broaden Thinking About Family Relationships (Family Dynamics, 2018).

My stories and advice are not referenced from episodes of the *Brady Bunch*, but are still filled with personal struggle, hard lessons, hope, revelation, truth, and triumph. Please note that this book is about me and what I learned about myself and my role as somebody's STEPFATHER (STEPDAD). Hopefully, the words and pictures in this book will encourage, equip, strengthen, and empower those MEN (and the WOMEN who love an adore them), to fully embrace the challenges, blessings, honor, and privileges associated with being somebody's STEPFATHER (STEPDAD). **Always Show Up! & Show Out! God is Watching!**

THE GREATEST STEPFATHER IN HISTORY

If **YOU** ever get discouraged or weary, as somebody's STEPFATHER (STEPDAD), but YOU know that YOU are doing God's work in your family, do not give up because it feels ridiculous and is very hard. Just think about the Pressure and Responsibility of the most famous STEPFATHER (STEPDAD) in the History of the World.

> <u>Isaiah 7:14</u> - Therefore the Lord himself shall give you a sign; Behold, a virgin shall conceive, and bear a son, and shall call his name Immanuel.
>
> <u>Matthew 1:18-25</u> - Now the birth of Jesus Christ was on this wise: When as his mother Mary was espoused to Joseph, before they came together, she was found with child of the Holy Ghost.
>
> <u>Matthew 1:20</u> - But while he thought on these things, behold, the angel of the Lord appeared unto him in a dream, saying, Joseph, thou son of David, fear not

to take unto thee Mary thy wife: for that which is conceived in her is of the Holy Ghost.

Matthew 2:13-15 - And when they were departed, behold, the angel of the Lord appeareth to Joseph in a dream, saying, Arise, and take the young child and his mother, and flee into Egypt, and be thou there until I bring thee word: for Herod will seek the young child to destroy him.

Matthew 2:19-23 - But when Herod was dead, behold, an angel of the Lord appeareth in a dream to Joseph in Egypt,

Luke 2:7 - And she brought forth her firstborn son, and wrapped him in swaddling clothes, and laid him in a manger; because there was no room for them in the inn.

Mark 6:3 - Is not this the carpenter, the son of Mary, the brother of James, and Joses, and of Juda, and Simon? and are not his sisters here with us? And they were offended at him.

YEAR 1

> "Every man shall bear his own burdens."
> **Galatians 6:5**

"I am "Mr. Sederick!"

I was born Sederick (Se-d-er-ick) Charles Rice to the late Shirley Ann (Spears) Rice and Charles Rice on a hot summer day in August. Even though my real name has multiple syllables, I grew up pronouncing my first name phonetically Sedrick with an S, two Es, and a K. For some reason, I would tell people the "E" in my name was silent. When I traveled as an adult to San Francisco, California, I was told by a street vendor that my name means "Prince" in Arabic. When I opened my eyes on the day of my birth, my name was "Dwight," but my Father objected since his name was not a part of my name and forced an immediate change. My Aunt Loretta suggested that my first name would be Sederick, based on how she spelled it. Many people to this day still try to put me in the "Cedric" or "Sedrick" name club, which I quickly, but humorously correct. 1972 was a very good year for me, as a newborn. Some top R&B songs on my birthday were:

1. *I'm Still in Love With You* by Al Green
2. *Power of Love* by Joe Simon
3. *Too Late To Turn Back Now* by Cornelius Brothers & Sister Rose
4. *Where is The Love,* by Roberta Flack & Donny Hathaway
5. *I Miss You (Part I)* by Harold Melvin And The Blue Notes

Aunt Loretta

Music has been important to me, from a very young age, especially the song, *You'll Never Find a Love Like Mine* (1976), by Lou Rawls. This was the first song I remember hearing and seeing on *Soul Train*, an American music-dance television program created and executively produced by Don Cornelius, which aired from October 2, 1971 until March 27, 2006 (Soul Train, 2020). I also embraced the Classics, including *Ludwig van Beethoven's 5 Symphony* (1804-1808), which I heard during a music appreciation class in the 5th grade. One of my other favorites was *Mama Used to Say* (1982) by Junior Giscombe. I did not understand how powerful the lyrics were for my life, and others at that time, but now clearly understand the lessons in the song.

My Mother was born under the sign of Taurus and her firm guidance was very much a part of my growth and development from childhood to adulthood. She was a true "Bull," because she was smart, ambitious, trustworthy, stubborn, honest, trailblazing, unwavering, reliable, understanding, stable, persistent, and hard-working. My Father was born under the sign of Aries and thus, I credit my sense of logic, intellect, morals, and principles to my learning from his approach to life. He was always a "Ram in the Bush" for me with an independent, generous, optimistic, courageous, and enthusiastic approach to problem-solving. He could be moody, short-tempered, impulsive, and impatient. I do not ever remember my parents living together. They divorced when I was two years of age, but I was still blessed to have a Mother and Father in my life who guided me with unconditional love.

I grew up in my Mother's house and under her rules and regulations. I had my own room, but without a door. There was no need to have any privacy in the house, since I was not paying any of the bills and of course my Mother reminded me of that weekly. We were very close and often listened to Blues together.

Momma

Daddy

Her favorite song was *The Blues Is Alright* (1984) by Little Milton, often called the International Blues Anthem by songwriters, artists, and people around the world. We discussed mental health issues, the benefit of counseling, depression, and she always prepared me for her death by saying 'I'm not going to always be here." When I was growing up, my Mother and her brothers and sisters would always talk about being "nervous" and that their "nerves were bad," which meant they were tired and out of patience. I also learned and heard about "nervous breakdowns" early in my life. There were no fancy terms then to describe what were "periods of intense mental distress associated with anxiety, depression, and acute stress disorder that could cause someone to lose the ability to cope with life's challenges (Scaccia, 2019).

My Mother dealt with mental illness most, if not all of her adult life, but she was strong and taught me to seek counseling. She even took me with her to counseling, at the Southeast Arkansas Mental Health Center. She would call it the Mental Health Center. I vividly remember one session where the counselor, using a blue toy car, told me at a very young age to "never let anyone drive my blue car." He was giving me instructions for my life, and teaching me that I should be in control of my thoughts, emotions, feelings, attitudes, and goals. The counselor's words, and my Mother's actions, set the stage for me to seek counseling as an adult, to talk things out, write things out, and work things out to fix the problems in my life.

My Mother was a smoker and loved Kool Filter Kings (Menthol). At that time, I could walk to the corner store and buy a pack for $1.00. The store owners knew that I was not going to try to smoke the cigarettes and was just running an errand for an adult in my family. My Mother smoked a lot and then one day abruptly just STOPPED! No counseling, no substitute, no plan. She just STOPPED using one of the most addictive substances (Nicotine) on the planet. I knew then that she was a Strong Black Woman and my Momma. I also knew my Mother loved me, but we often clashed because I was young, anxious, impatient, hard-headed, and stubborn. We also clashed because as much as I loved her, I really wanted to spend more time with my Father, as a young man searching for my male identity.

My Mother eventually grew tired of my behavior, when I turned 18, and insisted that I go to live with my Father (told me to get out). "There is nothing like a strong Black Momma that sacrifices for their children, loves them dearly, but has no problem telling them to get their (tail) out of her house!" I was excited to move across town (West Side to the North Side) but didn't know I would have to learn some new rules and regulations, as it related to dealing with an Aries male and becoming a man. My Father was a very disciplined man, with specific rules for living, working, and even interacting with people and animals. One time a stray cat began stopping by our house for food and my Father began feeding it. The cat would hang around and eventually made the front porch its home.

We would often go to get cat food and leave it where we knew the cat would show up. One day I asked my Father if he were going to feed the cat. He said "No! Today is Tuesday, and I only feed the cat on Mondays and Fridays. The cat has to hunt, kill some mice or rats and find its own food on those other days!" My Father had given the cat rules by which to live its life if it wanted some food from him. I was amazed at how he approached that situation, but it was another reminder of how my Father always applied his rules of living, and had no problem teaching even a stray cat those rules. I thought that approach was ridiculous until I saw the cat only on Mondays and Fridays.

My Father was also a practical man, who liked all kinds of music by artists such as Bob Dylan, Howling Wolf, Johnny Cash, Muddy Waters, Bo Diddley, B.B. King, and Bobby Rush. When we rode together in his white Toyota truck going from the Flea Market to Wabbaseka, Arkansas, we would listen to songs like *I'm a Man* (1967) by Bo Diddley, Muddy Waters & Little Walter, *Little Red Rooster* (1962) by Howlin' Wolf, *How Blue Can You Get?* (1964) by B.B. King, and Hen Pecked (1995), *I Ain't Studdin' You* (2003), and *Porcupine Meat* (2016) by Pine Bluff, Arkansas Blues Legend Bobby Rush. We also listened to songs by Johnny Cash, a legend and famous Arkansan from Kingsland, Arkansas, world-renowned singer, and songwriter of country music.

Wabbaseka, Arkansas

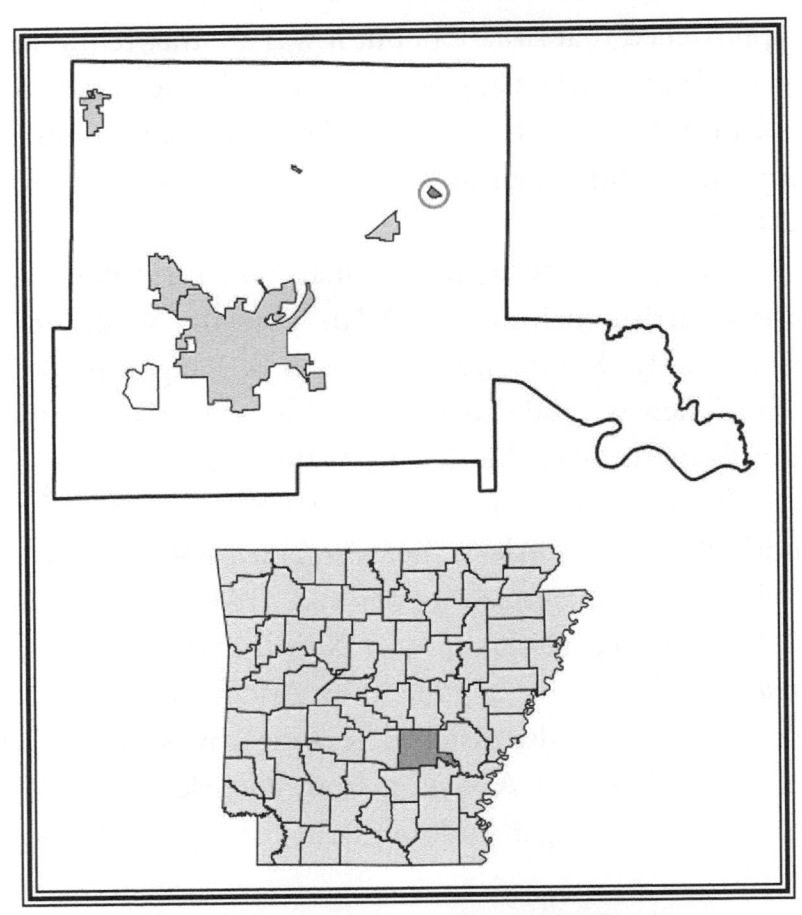

Figure 1. Schematic of locator map of Wabbaseka, Arkansas (Wabbaseka, 2020)

This is how and when I began to shape my views on the role of a MAN or MEN in relationships, families, education, work, and in life. My Father really liked radio programs and we often listened to *Coast to Coast AM*, which was a radio show broadcast (1:00 a.m.- 5:00 a.m.). Their hosts Art Bell, George Noory, George Knapp, and their guests, discussed paranormal activities, conspiracy theories, climate change, crop circles, extraterrestrials, quantum physics, hauntings, and many other scary topics (Coast to Coast AM, 2020).

One of my favorite television shows was *Sanford and Son*, a sitcom that aired on NBC from January 14, 1972, to March 25, 1977. This show starred Redd Foxx and Desmond Wilson, who were junk dealers. I saw my relationship with my Father, as a reflection of the episodes of that show. We often exchanged and sold "junk, antiques, and collectibles," at the local Flea Market and argued a lot, but I had to admit that my Father was the wisest and most disciplined man I had ever met. I also learned and mimicked other men in my family (Grandfathers and uncles), male figures in my friends' families, male teachers, pastors, and deacons.

According to **Erik Erikson's Stages of Psychosocial Development**, at this time in my life, I was in the (Adolescence) Identity vs. Confusion 5th stage of ego, quickly moving into the 6th stage of ego (Young Adulthood) Intimacy vs. Isolation (Cherry, 2005). I did not know at the time, but that simply meant I was developing a sense of self, relied heavily on social relationships, and when I failed or made mistakes, I developed low self-esteem. As I moved into young adulthood, I insecurely developed loving relationships that failed, which often led to loneliness and isolation. I was still blessed to have an opportunity to learn from a community of men, while working summers at my Grandfather's (Victor Rice) automotive shop. This was my Father's idea after watching me sit around for a week, after school ended, hanging out with my friends, running the air conditioner all day, and eating up all the low-priced slightly blemished Tyson chicken.

I worked and learned in my Grandfather's shadow, just like my Father did, and always felt "young" in the presence of older men, as I listened to their conversations about work, WOMEN, bills, and life. My impatience for respect got the best of me one day when I got tired of feeling like the "kid." I asked my Grandfather when he was going to call me a MAN! He looked closely into my eyes and with a calm and light voice said, "I will call YOU a MAN when YOU become ONE!" (1990). That was the end of that, but that conversation set the stage for the next twenty years of my life to work hard to become, and be recognized as a MAN! I also wanted to be someone who was educated, an authoritarian, defined as "something or someone who has complete, or almost complete, control over one or more people" (Oh My!), works hard, loves his family, pays all the bills, and is the BOSS! My MAN mold cast was now set. I was ready for the world of work and relationships, or so I thought!

Over the next twenty years (1990-2010), that MAN persona took some Ls (Social Media Slang) that highlight extreme mistakes and circumstances, misunderstandings, frustration, suffering losses, and discomfort because things did not go as I had planned. The negative traits of my LEO sign often confused my decision-making abilities and views on life. While others saw me as arrogant, controlling, but also needy and insecure, I felt I was doing the best that could ever be done. **(Feel Free to Laugh Loudly from a Healthy Place)** as the great comedian, Katt Williams would say. This is also a time in my life when I began to understand the impact of multiple intelligences on how I reach and teach my students and how people see and interact with me.

Multiple intelligences are another way to "define and explain my intellect," and are usually used by teachers or instructors within their classroom work (pedagogy) (Cerruti, 2013). The *Theory of Multiple Intelligences* was first presented by Harvard Psychologist, Howard Gardner in his book entitled *Frames of the Mind: The Theory of Multiple Intelligences* (Gardner, 1983). In it, Gardner theorized that there are eight distinct intelligences that explain the abilities and talents of people (Gardner, 1983), which can also "help You better understand your own strengths" (Cerruti, 2013). The lists of intelligences include: Visual-Spatial, Linguistic Verbal, Logical-Mathematical, Bodily-Kinesthetic, Musical, Interpersonal, Intrapersonal, and Naturalistic (Types of Intelligence, 2017). Each Intelligence Type highlights the strength of the individual, characteristics, and also provides information on the best potential career choices (Types of Intelligence, 2017).

The more I read about Multiple Intelligences for my role as an educator, the more I became interested in how those intelligences impacted my roles as StepFather/StepDaddy in this blended family. I took a simple Multiple Intelligence test and discovered that I did have multiple intelligences with my strongest being Linguistic-Verbal, then Musical, followed by Logical Mathematical, and finally Interpersonal. People with Linguistic-Verbal intelligences can use words effectively in writing and speaking, use humor when telling stories (Interesting), and typically choose careers as writers, lawyers, or teachers (Types of Intelligence, 2017). I expected to have a Musical Intelligence based on my love for Music and experiences in marching bands. People in this category enjoy singing and playing musical instruments, can remember songs and melodies, and typically do well as singers, composers, or music teachers (Types of Intelligence, 2017). My Logical-Mathematical Intelligence score was no surprise to me because I often think about numbers ($$), like to analyze problems, and enjoy conducting scientific experiments. I tried early on to conduct several experiments in my blended family, with the approach that my hypothesis for the solution to every scenario, would be proven correct. Of course, that was never the case! There were too many variables out of my immediate control to calculate and for which to be responsible. (If YOU watched "Star Trek," during any season, that last statement will make sense).

My Interpersonal Intelligence score was interesting because these individuals are skilled at assessing the emotions and motivations, desires, and intentions of others (Sternberg, 2012). Wow! People with Interpersonal Intelligence can communicate well verbally, are skilled at non-verbal communication, see situations from different perspectives and usually choose careers as psychologists, philosophers, salespersons, or politicians (Types of Intelligence, 2017). Now that I have this knowledge, let us see how this all plays out over the next few chapters. I can honestly say right now, that some of the information from my intelligence test may have been in me, but I had not seen it yet. The other point that is interesting is that of all the careers highlighted by each Multiple Intelligence, I never saw a parent listed. (Interesting). Maybe that was God's intent of my Blended Family Experiment and Experience. I did feel as if I were on an assignment, but not really sure about how I felt about that.

Back to the story....

I should have seen changes in my life coming, but I was too full of myself to prepare. I had to be humbled several times and God placed me in a "Wilderness Season" from 2003-2010. Most people go through regular trials and tribulations as a part of life, but when God puts YOU in a "Wilderness Season," that experience is designed to extract "or draw out; to pull out; or to remove forcibly from a fixed position" **(Extract, 2020)** something in your character or circumstance that must be changed. For me, as big as I thought I was, I watched in slow motion as my life flipped and began to spin out of control. This was really strange and unusual to me because I was on top of the world, I had just earned a Ph.D., was featured in EBONY Magazine *"Young Leaders of the Future Under 30,"* had a new car, and a high-paying government job in Washington, D.C. The truth is, God grew tired of me taking all the credit for the success I had achieved, as I conveniently forgot to acknowledge his Grace & Mercy through my life process.

On that faithful day, I sat in my workplace cubicle confused, disheveled, and mad because my name was left off of the doctoral graduation program. A still, but firm voice, spoke to me and explained why that happened. It took me a while to recognize my "Burning Bush" moment, without the Bush, as I pleaded for forgiveness. I tried to convince God that I understood and learned my lesson and would fix whatever wrong I had done. The voice (God) said "YOU denied me for 7 years (1996-2003), so now I am going to deny YOU for 7 years."

I didn't believe it at first until my lifestyle, personality, finances, sanity, relationships, job, and peace were disrupted with no end in sight. I had no more government job. I gave the car back because I could not afford it or the insurance. I had to move out of my 1BR apartment into rented rooms in homes from Accokeek to Bowie, Maryland. I tried to find work, but had no other choice than to become a high school science teacher (as the voice of God said I had to do) earning half ($30,000 of my real salary $60,000, because I was not "certified" to teach. Now the MAN, that I wanted to be, had to stand up, show up, and show out under duress.

This was a necessary transition in my life. I am glad (In Retrospect) that it happened because I had to be held accountable for my actions, recognize and never forget the gift of Grace & Mercy given to me. If God wanted to use me, I had to change, and as usual, I was the kind of person who required several hard and sustained lessons to bring about that change. God was true to His Word and said "He would never leave me nor forsake me." In 2009, my Mother passed away and in 2010, things began to change. I received a call about a job opening at my Alma Mater, the University of Arkansas at Pine Bluff (UAPB), for an assistant professor position. I was still woozy, weary, dazed, and weathered after coming out of the "Wilderness Season," but ready for new opportunities.

What was my first objective? I was ready to mingle and date with a purpose, but I wanted to be decisive and very selective. After the last 15 years in schools and jobs, I was anxious and looking for a woman with no big hang ups, little to no emotional baggage, someone not impacted by past relationships, someone to put me on that high pedestal and give me all the attention and praise I needed. She also needed to be a beautiful, fun, outgoing Christian woman with no children. **(Feel Free to Laugh Loudly from a Healthy Place)**. I only put some of my non-negotiables in the "Looking For" search profile.

Sederick Charles Rice (2011): "I don't want to date or marry any woman with children. I think online dating though, can help me with that."

Charles Rice (2011): "Yeah! Well…."

Sederick Charles Rice (2014): "Daddy, you just don't understand the struggles I go through to maintain and support my family as a STEPFATHER (STEPDAD)." "I just need to borrow $5,000 today!" "Why don't you listen to me and just understand that?"

Charles Rice (2014): "I hear you, but I was smart enough not to get into a situation, where I needed to borrow $5,000 to take care of my family!"

Charles Rice (2014): "You have dug a hole for yourself that I can't see you getting out of."

Sederick Charles Rice (2014): "I know! I know! I know! When can we go down to Simmons Bank and get that $5,000? "I promise I'll pay you back on a monthly schedule!"

Charles Rice (2014): "Ahh!!!"

The online dating service was very effective in bringing new online opportunities for me to quickly meet a woman, date that woman, and then marry that woman, who had children. (I purposely left the name of the dating site out of the book because I am sure they would not appreciate any free advertising and knowledge of any successful testimonies). I think my personal dating profile was full of flattering words, humor and honesty and I was clear about what I wanted (except the "no children" part). I tried to paint a picture of achievable hopes and dreams for meaningful short or long-term companionship. Whatever it was, it worked. By 2011, I was married and adjusting to a new life, with a new job, new wife with children who liked me <u>some,</u> while I dated their Mother, but now viewed me differently. I heard secondhand, from the Mother, that the son said, "I like him!" This was great and all the motivation I needed.

    I really take things to heart and if you ever ask me to do anything, I try to put forth maximum effort. This can become very annoying during times when it really does not take all of that, but I started this book being honest about me. With that being said, I had done my part and made the ultimate personal, spiritual, and financial commitment to a woman with children. The only thing left was for me to receive my greatest honor, from the children, and to be recognized and called Daddy! The simple definition of Daddy is "One's Father or the oldest, best, or biggest example of something." You can probably tell from my Leo personality that the bolder the description of me, the more I liked and embraced it.

    What I did not know, and probably did not care about, was that the children were already in shock that their Mother married a man from Pine Bluff, who appeared to be anxious to be somebody's Daddy. I was ready to be put on that pedestal and take on all of the responsibilities of family. I was prepared to lead and instill the discipline, direct the present and future activities of the family, and sit on the "Mighty Throne of Wisdom," as everyone around me sought my magnificent advice and counsel. I am being dramatically descriptive, which I have the option to be, but YOU get the point. (This became all about me). The family dynamic changed, slowly over Year 1, as we all spent more time together, took trips, and awkwardly tried to setup up ground rules for our interactions. I waited to not only hear, but feel the reverential power of my role in the family as the Daddy, Protector, and Provider (See My LEO Traits). On another faithful day, when my patience had run out and I presented the children with an ultimatum, I learned a very valuable lesson. They appreciated my effort, but to them, **I am "Mr. Sederick."**

YEAR 2

> "Can a woman forget her nursing child, that she should have no compassion on the son of her womb? Even these may forget, yet I will not forget you."
>
> **Isaiah 49:15**

"We Knew Momma, Before You!"

According to Surviving and Thriving in Stepfamily Relationships: What Works and What Doesn't by Dr. Patricia L. Papernow (2013), there are 5 major challenges to blended families. 1) Insider/Outsider Positions are Intense and Stuck, 2) Children Struggle with Losses, Loyalty Binds, and Too Much Change, 3) Parenting Tasks Polarize the Adults, 4) Creating a New Family Culture, and 5) Ex-Spouses are Part of the Family (Papernow, 2013). I learned while reading this book about the different parenting leadership styles (Authoritative, Authoritarian, and Permissive). I had already chosen to be an Authoritarian, which is a style that emphasizes "do what I say do, because I said so." I guess I have to credit my Mother for that kind of parenting attitude.

I learned early in my life to "stay in a child's place," and limit negotiations when given instructions. For my new situation, I felt "This is how things are going to go and that is it!) I clearly did not know what I was doing, but my idea to jump right in and take charge seemed just **Feeling Insecure Needing Esteem** (FINE!) According *to Maslow's Hierarchy of Needs*, which is a motivational theory in the field of psychology (McCleod, 2020), I was right between *Esteem* and *Self-Actualization*, at this point in my blended family life, which meant I was over the place trying to lead, but at the same time needed people to allow me to lead. The Leo Man was also pressing for recognition so the more I pushed, the more I got push back.

Then it happened! I was blessed with another child, which now changed my perspective and Stepdaddy/Daddy ratio to 3. I went from 0 to 3 children in the last year and a half. My response was, of course, to become more engaged with the older children, as I wrapped my mind around my extended Fatherhood role. I still wanted that "Daddy," title, but it was cool to be Mr. Sederick because now I was going to show the older children why I deserved the "Daddy" title. This meant I was going to be "real extra" and my efforts were competitive in nature. I do not know with whom I was competing; I guess probably the older children, but my drive was to demonstrate, as often I as could, that I was "Stepping In and Stepping Up."

My Wife was recovering from childbirth, so she needed her rest. I was trying to bond and operate "my program," to get my esteem needs up and move into self-actualization. There was friction and I do not remember how it happened, but somehow every aspect of "my program" was not embraced by the older children. We spent time together, but I still felt like an outsider, so my natural response was to be "more extra" I began reading *Dare To Be A Man: The Truth Every Man Must Know... and Every Woman Needs to Know About Him* by David G. Evans (Evans, 2010). I focused on the Art of Verbal Contemplation to improve my communication skills with the older children.

I believed that a more strategic approach would get me the results I was looking for by being **C**lear, **C**onsistent, **C**aring, **C**lean, and **C**onfrontational (Evans, 2010). The goal was to speak clearly, listen carefully, and then comprehend what was said. I have always spoken more than I listened, and in a situation where not much is being said, I missed a lot. Another strategy from David Evans' book was to develop mutual submission, which improves the success of love, respect, honor, and dignity in a relationship (Evans, 2010).

An issue for me was feeling that submitting meant a loss of authority as the StepFather/Daddy of the family.

I need authority! I felt the children should submit to me, because I am the adult and I am working "my program," to bring everyone in this unit to an understanding of my vision for their future. My authoritarian approach kicked back in and verbal contemplation with the children broke down. I could not go to my wife or Mother-in-law for advice. Why would I do this? I am going to figure this out on my own! As the responsibilities of a newborn increased, my attentions and intentions changed toward the older children. They were still a major factor in the success of this family, but I could not figure out why I was not getting the fictional level of recognition that I felt I deserved.

Things changed for me financially, due to the needs of a family of 4, so I had to work more and spread myself thinly over multiple jobs. My thought was, at least I could be the Provider and thus, the older children would have no choice but to embrace me as the true leader. I knew what I was doing, and it was going to work. As my wife recovered, she began to regain her status in the family,(as if she ever lost it), and operated with a direct, but calm demeanor. She was getting results from the older children, and for some reason, I did not understand that.

What was so different about my approach and hers? Why were the older children so receptive to her thoughts and wishes, but often ignored my efforts? (Yes, I was really thinking about a question that had an obvious answer) Was I being jealous? What was I missing? I am a scientist and I have gone through the Scientific Method in this family experiment, so things should be working in my favor by now. Was I being petty? Was I being ridiculous? I did not think so. I was just being me and ready to continue taking charge of this and all situations in this family. I eventually found a brief balance and began to make gains and progress. If I did not have responsibility with the older children, I made responsibilities with them through activities, family movie nights, and R.L. Stine Goosebumps' episodes.

My expectation was that I would receive my due honor very soon. This worked for a while, until I was building visible momentum. I was on it and did not miss a beat. I was providing, present, and focused on the needs and wants of the family. If they needed anything, I would get it immediately. Even if I had to borrow the money to do so. I was not going to be outdone. Never! I believed I had figured this thing out and the family unit was moving into a positive direction, in my favor. I had worked hard to get to this point and the older children could see my influence was increasing. I do not know if it were their "Tween Spidey Sense" or whether they had perfect timing, but as close as I was to reaching self-actualization, they threw me a curveball. Almost in concert and at the same time, they told me "We Knew Momma Before You!" I heard it, but didn't really understand what they said at first, until they repeated it. "We Knew Momma Before You!"

I understood their words the second time more clearly, but was confused as to why they would say that to me. How did their, knowing my wife before me have anything to do with me? I dismissed what they were saying because it made no sense to me. What was the point of that? What was the purpose of that statement? I was doing very well up until that point and now another setback. I was the adult in the situation, but my response was to be petty, competitive, argumentative, and "in my feelings." The older children had drawn a line in the sand with their Mother, which was their right to do, with somebody else, just not me.

After almost two years of working at this, I felt I had earned the right to be on the team. For them, I was still in the "rookie" stage of the family and they were smart enough to know that they had more history with my wife, than I did. They played their Joker card like professional card players in a Spades game, where they cut my Ace of Hearts, took one of my books, and "set" my team. (Think About It!) What else was I supposed to do, but get mad and reserve the right to pull out all of my negative Leo traits and get deeper into my own feelings? It seemed like a good idea to me, but in response, they doubled down about their relationship with their Mother. Why am I competing with these children? All I could do was get madder and more defensive. I forgot my verbal communication training, from the David Evans' book (Evans, 2010), as he highlighted a very important scripture for such a time as this.

> Wherefore, my beloved brethren, let every man be swift to hear, slow to speak, slow to wrath. **James 1:19**

I did the opposite of the wisdom in that scripture and made it my mission to engage! The truth is they did know their Mother before I came into the picture, as I became more defensive in my approach to try to secure my role in this family unit. I had an idea to fix it all. My next move will be more dramatic and direct. The children may have known their Mother before me, but now they were going to get to know Mr. Sederick who is going "flex" as Husband, Father, Stepfather, Leader, and Head of this family. Believe That!

YEAR 3

> "For if a man think himself to be something, when he is nothing, he deceiveth himself." **Galatians 6:3**

"I Have To Be Boss To Make This Work!"

I learned late in this parenting experience the value of understanding one's love language. When the concept of a Love Language was finally introduced to me, I was already full steam ahead working in my limited understanding of family leadership. *The 5 Love Languages: The Secret to Love That Lasts* by Gary Chapman (Chapman, 2015), was a great resource for me to identify and understand the value of Love Languages within relationships. Knowledge such as "The object of love is not getting something **YOU** want, but doing something for the well-being of the one **YOU** love," "Encouragement requires empathy and seeing the world from your spouse's perspective," and the error of "Bringing into today the failures of yesterday while polluting a potentially wonderful present" (Chapman, 2015). I did some reading and was more familiar with the impact of Words of Affirmation, Quality Time, Receiving Gifts, Acts of Service, and Physical Touch Love Languages.

Unfortunately, familiarity of a subject is not enough to guarantee success in practice. As described in *Chapter 9: Discovering Your Primary Love Language* "Ignoring love languages is like ignoring the needs of a garden: if we don't weed, water or fertilize, it will die a slow death and if one abuses or manipulates love languages- It is like taking a machete to that same garden and chopping everything up" (Chapman, 2015). (Deep!). I took an online Love Languages quiz and discovered that my primary love language is Words of Affirmation, followed by Physical Touch, and then Acts of Service. This, of course, explains a lot about me and my personality, but this is recent knowledge and I had no idea of how to identify or use this information as I began Year 3.

I was prepped and ready to begin "Operation I Run This!", with the attention to detail I gave my academic studies with one goal in mind-WIN! My targets were a Mother-In-Law, Wife, and 3 Children. (**YOU** already know what is going to happen, but I will explain what I did and what happened in Year 3 anyway). (**Feel Free to Laugh Loudly from a Healthy Place**).

My first objective was to be more involved in the decision-making in the family and to get the RESPECT I deserve for being the MAN. I wanted to be consulted and involved in "all" matters big and small. I made time and it was my goal to ask, verify, inquire, follow-up, review, and document all family goings- on. I was still adjusting financially from being responsible for four people, so I had two jobs and worked days and nights. That did not matter. I wanted to know everything, before it happened, and if there were a small space of time that I felt I was out of the loop, I would "trpp." Trppin' (1980s term) did not mean being high on psychedelic drugs, that was Tripping. Trppin' meant freaking out, acting a fool without thinking or being erratic. Wait! That's really the same thing. Anyway, back to the story. Mr. Sederick wanted to be more engaged in that "family business." It didn't take my family long to recognize that something had changed in me.

My first test was keeping up with, and participating in, "all" of the extracurricular activities of the older children. Picking up and dropping off was the name of the game, and I did not want any help. This would help the children and me to bond. I had a few opportunities to be a "Soccer" Dad, but all that expected conversation and bonding, during the drives, did not happen. Most times, I would get a call from my Wife or Mother-in-law checking in on me to make sure I had done what I said I was going to do; Arrive on time! Pick the children up and drop them off safely! I didn't know why they kept checking on me (I know now), I am the MAN! I got this! Eventually, all of that runnin' around got to me. I was so weary and tired of the schedule and calls to make sure I didn't miss a pick-up or drop off. I know my Wife and Mother-in-law were probably discussing and laughing at the fact that I wanted more responsibility, while already struggling with my current tasks. That is a symptom of not knowing and understanding what you are doing. I was really "biting off more than I could chew." My PRIDE would not allow me to admit that 1) they were better at this than me because they had been managing families longer, and 2) both of them were experienced Mothers. I just do not know why I missed that understanding (**YOU** know why I missed it.) long story short, I had to resign from my full-time Soccer Dad duty, so I could spend the rest of my time working multiple jobs to be a PROVIDER. (Lesson Learned)

The second test was for me to adjust and modify the family holiday visitation schedule (Think About It!). In any marriage or blended family, there will be negotiations about where the family will spend Thanksgiving, Christmas, New Year's Eve/Day, Mother's Day, Father's Day, and Easter. My blended family was no different and my feeling and belief were that "all" those holidays should be reserved for what I want to do and ME! I think I actually said that, one time, as my wife rolled her eyes while she was singing to and burping a baby. The older children were not interested in my vision for holidays. They already had family routines and holiday traditions in place and here I was changing things up. I thought this was a very good strategy for "Operation I Run This!"

Truth be told, I really did not spend a lot of time with my own extended family during the holidays, because I really do not like holidays. I think it is because the banks are closed, and the mail does not run. I was going to force my new blended family unit to spend holidays the way I wanted. Before we got into that, it was already a no-go, I forgot that the older children had a voice and preferences. I quickly realized that they were more comfortable with familiar family members, which makes sense. (I was still annoyed). The other thing I realized was that my Mother-in-law and Wife were very close and always together on holidays, so if they were together, the children were always with them. Where was I going to be? (**YOU** already know). Why was I even considering changing my position? Did I change my position or was my position changed for me? I know what I did, I told myself that this is what is "best for the children" and that "any rules and regulations I made up regarding the holiday visitation schedule would be postponed to a later date." (See how I made myself feel better, without admitting that I was doing too much). This new approach actually worked because we did, as a blended family, eventually rotate visitations, during the major holidays. I was surprised at how a little give and take on my part made things much better. The problem with forcing anything, especially in a blended family, is the risk of losing flexibility, common ground, understanding, teachable moments, opportunities, and trust. (Lesson Learned (LLs).

The third and most difficult test during "Operation I Run This!" was for me to establish myself as MAN and BOSS in the family to my Mother-In-Law. (Please Go Get Your Popcorn). My Mother passed away in 2009, so by this time, I did not have that Motherly voice and wisdom to help me understand that I was about to jump into some deep water. I admit I was gambling, taking risky action, and placing a bet on my own skills and abilities for the prize (Whatever that was). I can hear my Mother's sweet loud direct voice now saying "Boy! Are YOU stupid!" And just like the lyrics from that classic song by Kenny Rogers, The Gambler (1978), I had to learn when to hold, fold, and walk away. Now I started the **Mother-In-Law I Run This Challenge**. My goal was to convince somebody else's Mother that I was GREAT! And IN CHARGE! **(Feel Free to Laugh Loudly from a Healthy Place)**.

YOU are probably wondering how I even began this futile process. I used past events as my motivation. I was still probably mad that when I first met and was dating my Wife, as a result of an online dating service, my Mother-in-law secretly scouted out my name and appeared to have run several criminal background checks on me. I felt this way because she knew a lot about my background **(Feel Free To Laugh Loudly from a Healthy Place)**. I really did not know then why I was the subject of such intrusive scrutiny (I know now but keep reading and **YOU** will learn later). I had a doctorate degree, recently published my second book *Four Tubas, a Guitar, and Gallery of Cheerleaders: Transition in the Life of a Black Ph.D.*, was working, and had a "Fair" credit score.

Four Tubas, a Guitar, and a Gallery of Cheerleaders
Transition in the Life of a Black Ph.D
A First Person Narrative
Sederick C. Rice

Foreword by Pastors Marc and Nanette Buntin
World Impact Christian Center
9601 Ardwick Ardmore Road
Springdale, MD 20774

Illustration 2: Book Cover from Four Tubas a Guitar and Gallery of Cheerleaders: *Transition in the Life of a Black Ph.D.* **(Rice, 2010)**

Slowly over time, I began competing (again), this time with my Mother-in-law, for attention, recognition, praise, adoration, and connection with my wife and the children. I viewed my Mother-in-law as the final obstacle to convincing the rest of the family that I was here to stay and should be respected accordingly. My strategy was very simple. I would do everything she had already been doing, but do it better. (Here we go again). I tried to take charge of the affairs of an older woman, who still was holding out on believing that I was a good fit for her daughter and this family, and then expect lots of "Good Jobs and Thank Yous." I told **YOU** my negative Leo traits are a "trpp." As I became more aggressive in my decision-making, she became more strategic in her approach. She already had the confidence of my wife, (her daughter), and my children,(her grandchildren), but I persisted anyway. She tolerated me for a while as I tried to establish myself as a disciplinarian. The more the children confidently pushed back against my instructions and commands, the more I tried to give more instruction and commands.

Speaking fairly and honestly, my Mother-in-law is an honest God-Fearing Woman and she was supportive. I just wanted her to recognize me as LEADER and BOSS! (That is All!) Most stereotypical marriage narratives, for many MEN, include a section about the evil Mother-in-law that wreaks havoc in the family to the frustration of the Husband and Father/Stepfather. I knew what I was trying to do, but my Mother-in-law recognized and was confident in what she had already done. She was "Nanny", as well as the matriarch of the family and was present for everyone's birth in the family, except mine. As a God-Fearing Woman, and active member and Church Mother in the greater body of the Church of God in Christ (COGIC) with keen and "seasoned" Mother Wit, she had POWER. That did not matter to me, because I still persisted just to make my point. "I Need to be the Boss of This Thing, for it to Work." I remember clearly that one evening we were all eating dinner at my Mother-in-law's house, and I was very chatty and probably annoyed by something the children were doing and I tried to correct it. I do not know how we got on this subject, but seemingly, out of the blue, my Mother-in-law said to me in front of everyone, "YOU don't tell me what to do!"

I was so stunned and speechless. Where did that come from, I wondered? (**YOU** know where that came from) My Mother would sometimes tell me that "I would argue with a sign that I painted myself!" (**Feel Free to Laugh Loudly from a Healthy Place**). I had no come back because I was just blindsided with raw honesty and truth. I think she felt that I was getting out of my lane a little bit, so she had to remind me of the "true" boundaries of this blended family relationship. A second incident occurred when I was frustrated with the children and I decided to call my Mother-in-law for some helpful advice. Yes, I was angry, I was dramatic, and I slipped and said, "They (the children) just make me not even want to deal with them, I'm tired of this!" My soft-spoken and gentle Mother-in-law raised her voice that day and yelled at me.

I do not even remember what she said, but whatever it was, it certainly got my attention. It was also like my Mother was speaking to me from heaven in the language she knew I understood best, which reminded me that I had been taught to "RESPECT My Elders." I immediately calmed down, changed and lowered my tone, and my Mother-in-law then gave me some wise and useful Motherly advice to help me to build a better relationship with the children. I appreciate those experiences because they really woke me up. Stress and working a lot, got my emotions all twisted up and it was only a matter of time before my Irrational, Needy, Egotistical side came out. Her ultimate goal will always be the safety, security, and wellbeing of her children, which includes my

Wife and grandchildren. She really did not care that I was "in my feelings" about this situation or any other, which is fair because as a MAN, I know my Mother would have said the same thing. My Mother-in-law patiently entertained my frustrations, vents and rants, but still took the time to help me see more clearly that my experiences were only the beginning of the work that I had to put in.

Sometimes as MEN, we get so focused on our plans, programs, visions, and objectives for the family that we forget there was always someone in place before we got there. As MEN, we want, and need to be leaders of the family, as outlined in the Bible, but the contributions of the Momma-Elders <u>must</u> be considered and honored. I learned in Year 3 that my Mother-in-law was, and still is, an important component to the success of my blended family. As quoted by many, "God gave YOU two ears and one mouth for a reason… Listen twice and speak once!" (Lesson Learned (LLs). I was now more open to constructive criticism (ridicule) and then toned down my aggression some. I still had that LEO PRIDE and wanted to demonstrate what I could do in this family, as the MAN.

YEAR 4

> "Do nothing out of selfish ambition or vain conceit. Rather, in humility value others above yourselves."
>
> **Philippians 2:3**

"Her Momma Can Help You, Deal With It!"

Mother Wit
Moth·er Wit
noun
1. natural ability to cope with everyday matters; common sense.
2. Inborn intelligence; Innate good sense

"Life doesn't come with a manual. It comes with a *Mother.*"

"Being a Mother is an attitude, not a biological relation"- **Robert A. Heinlein**

"A Mother is she who can take the place of all others but whose place no one else can take"- **Cardinal Meymillod**

"Mothers don't sleep. They just worry with their eyes closed."- **Nitya Prakash**

"The bond between Mothers and their children is one defined by love."- **President George W. Bush**

As a Mother's prayers for her children are unending, so are the wisdom, grace, and strength they provide to their children."- **President George W. Bush**

"Nothing is lost until your Mother can't find it."-**Unknown**

> "A Mother's love for her child is like nothing else in the world. It knows no law, no pity, it dares all things and crushes down remorselessly all that stands in its path"- **Agatha Christie**
>
> "A Mother's love is unending, unwavering & unconditional"- **Sandy Richards**

The most powerful verse of Shirley Caesar's song *No Charge*, for me was, "the full cost of my Love is no charge." The quotes and song lyrics, as an intro into Year 4, will set the stage for me to fully understand the power of a Mother's Love. This is very important because I know, as a MAN, I have a role to play as Husband, Father, and Stepdaddy, but the role of a Mother is critical to the success of any blended family. Below is a conversation I overheard while sitting in a barber chair getting a haircut.

Barber Shop (Pine Bluff, Arkansas)

> **Barber:** "What's going on?"
>
> **Waiting Customer:** "Nothing much, just working and living life."
>
> **Barber:** "Cool! How's the family?"

Waiting Customer: "They are good just trying to get some things done at the house and deal with these kids."

Barber: "I understand."

Waiting Customer: "I'm just dealing with my lady's parents." "They have been calling and asking if we needed any help with a bill or with the kids."

Barber: "That's Good!"

Waiting Customer: "Nope! Not to me.

Barber: "Why?"

Waiting Customer: "They are doing too much. I don't need their help, I got it!" The more they do, the more they want to be in our business."

Barber: "Bruh! You are going to miss out on your blessings. Accept the help with a bill here and there and let that pride go."

Waiting Customer: "Nah! I'm good! This is my family and I don't need their help!

As I sat in the barber chair listening to that dialogue, I had to reflect on my current life, and wondered if I ever felt like the waiting customer. Was I smarter than that? Were the waiting customer's feelings justified? Did I ever feel threatened by receiving help and assistance from my in-laws? What about my PRIDE? The answer to all those questions is, of course, YES. Year 4 is a summary of my emotions and efforts after the eye-opening talk with my Mother-in-law. As my Wife recovered and was now busy with all three children, I slowly realized the value of a Mother, Grandmother, and Nanny. I was still competing for attention and status in the family and what I thought was some level of RESPECT. My plan was to be the Superman of Providing, with a belief that I did not need help, and I still had something to prove. (We have been here before, so **YOU** know how this is going to play out.)

There were several things about my next set of plans that were already in place that would impact the outcome. I was still operating with emotional and historical boundaries and guidelines, but I had no instructions. I probably wouldn't have followed the instructions even if they were outlined in a quick read bullet point format. (**YOU** get my point). I was in a Blended Family Boot Camp, which can be defined from a military perspective as "a form of *Basic Training*", which prepares recruits for all elements of service: physically, mentally, and emotionally. It gives service members the basic tools necessary to perform the roles that would be assigned to them for the duration of the tour (Today's Military, 2020). Service boot camps for the United States Army last 10 weeks, for the Marine Corps 12 weeks, United States Navy 7-9 weeks, Air Force 7.5 weeks, and 8 weeks for the United States Coast Guard (Today's Military, 2020). Five interesting Boot Camp Facts:

> 1) Basic Training is an intense experience.
> 2) Basic Training is a tough process.
> 3) By enlisting **YOU** are contractually obligated to complete Boot Camp and serve.
> 4) The combination of physical training, field exercises, and classroom time makes individuals <u>Strong</u> and <u>Capable</u>.
> 5) If **YOU** find that **YOU** are incompatible with serving, **YOU** can receive an administrative discharge.

There are so many parallels between military training and the level of commitment required for success in blended families. I was still in Boot Camp in Year 4 (208 weeks) and whether I wanted to admit it or not, my Mother-in-law, Wife, and children were my drill instructors. I was still a recruit that was continuously learning, evaluated, corrected, mentored, and given instructions in the customs and practice of this blended family. My Mother-in-law was the lead drill instructor from whose standards I was always trying to exceed. (Does this sound familiar to YOU?) She was the most experienced, oldest, wisest, and most respected member of the family.

She was the Mother of the Mother of the children. Terms like *Big Momma, Nanna, Nanny, Grammy, Grandmother, MawMaw, Meme, G-MA,* and *Gigi* all illustrate the love and respect, from people around the world, afforded to a Mother of a Mother or Mother of a Father. My Mother-in-law was also, at a point in her life, where she had nothing more to prove to me or anyone else. I was still in the "prove and be recognized stage" and needed my efforts to be rewarded, documented, and shared (That is a Facebook reference). I also needed credit and appreciation for being such a wonderful hard-working and committed MAN.

The dynamic between my Mother-in-law and me was a unique one, because we viewed the world differently. She was a Baby Boomer (Born between 1946-1964), and I am Generation X (Born between 1965-1980). As I watched and studied how she cared for my wife when she was sick, after childbirth and surgeries, or when she was just not feeling well, I saw a veteran Mother who acted with a plan and purpose. (I tried to be mad, but I didn't know what to be mad about).

She was calm about the things which kept me up at night. She was completely cool under pressure and I just wondered how and if, I would ever be able to approach life that way. I wanted that ability to know what to do and when to do it, to make everything alright (Mother Wit). As a Baby Boomer, her generation pursued the "American Dream," and were extremely loyal to their children; trusted no one over 30 years of age; wanted to make a difference; and were driven workaholics with the goal to establish self-worth, identity, and fulfillment (West Midland Family Center, n.d.). As a member of Generation X, I was a latchkey kid, and a part of the first generation that would not do as well financially as their parents, self-reliant, possessed techno-literacy, fun, entrepreneurial, and suspicious of Baby Boomer values (West Midland Family, n.d.).

Baby Boomers were equipped to handle crisis, competent, competitive, often lived to work, and were loyal to their careers and employers-while Generation Xers were adaptable, confident, competent, results-driven, self-starters, and are often angry, but do not know why (West Midland Family Center, n.d.). As much as I wanted my Mother-in-law to see me in the light that I saw myself, her values, approach, concerns, and fears were totally different from mine. I did not, of course, recognize the generational gap between us. My Mother-in-law was old enough to be my Mother, but as Husband, Father, Stepfather, and Principal Provider (or so I thought), I wanted to be treated as an equal member of this blended family. Many of our interactions were funny because it appeared as though we were competing, with each other, until my financial circumstances tightened up quite a bit. Things got tough on me financially and just like the waiting customer at the barbershop, I would suffer before I asked for any help. PRIDE would make that option my absolute last choice, but God has a way of forcing **YOU** to change in the midst of the person or circumstances **YOU** face. I needed help! How could I be seen as an equal in this blended family (Which never was the case) if I asked for help?

The Bible tells me that I am the head of this family, but I did not realize at the time, that head does not mean BOSS; it means RESPONSIBLE! I also wanted my Wife and the children to adore me like they did their Nanny, and was a little jealous that that was just not happening. I believed that would help with my own personal and financial insecurities and struggles as well as help me to gain the footing in this blended family. (I needed to feel I was contributing.) I see now that the purpose of my Blended Family Boot Camp experience was to gain strength, improve my confidence, and transform into a MAN of Wisdom. I was working on another **P**repared for **H**igher **D**uty (PHD) and **P**atient **H**umble **D**addy (PHD) degree in this blended family, with the best teacher I could have, my Mother-in-law.

I believe in hard study and therefore watched more closely at her interactions with my wife and children and was amazed at the sacrifices she would make without concern or thought. My Mother-in-law had a few rules that she learned growing up as a member of COGIC. #1. "If **YOU** tell a child **YOU** are going to do something, keep your word and do it." #2. "If **YOU** buy a child something but get upset with them about being a child making mistakes and doing wrong, do not take those things away." This is where I struggled to connect with this kind of thinking, but I am not a Mother, so I am excused. I believed in blessing the children, but if they acted up, I would quickly take that same blessing away. I tried that a few times to try to make a point and to get the children to see things from my adult perspective, which is impossible. I had to remind myself that they are children and are going to mess up, which is a point where I can build a better relationship with them by teaching that some things are serious, while others are important, but not that serious. I learned that from my Mother-in-law, as I watched her give and provide and let her grandchildren put her through a rollercoaster of emotions.

My PRIDE weakened, as I realized that my Mother-in-law and I are not equals and will never be equals, then I was able to humbly ask for help with my marriage, raising children, and "dealing with those bills." It took me a long time to let that foolish PRIDE go and to stop competing with my own drill instructor, in this Blended Family Boot Camp. My Mother would say "**YOU** are cutting off your nose to spite your face!" This simply means that **YOU** should not do something that will cause more harm to **YOU** than to the person with whom **YOU** are angry; or do not let your overreaction lead to self-harm (Grammarist, n.d.).

During a recent Watch Night Service (Church Service 10:00 PM- 12:00 AM) that is designed to bring in the New Year), as a tradition of many African-American (Black) churches, my Mother-in-law stood up and made a powerful testimony about her life and family. She said, "I had a difficult pregnancy with my child and didn't know if she was going to make it, so I prayed and asked God if He would give me one, I would never ask for another." A Mother's Love has No Bounds. "How could I possibly compete with that?" She was trying to get me to understand, and begin practicing her level of "unconditional love," which can only be described as "giving affection without limitations and love without conditions," a Mother's Love. (Lesson Learned (LLs)

YEAR 5

> "Anyone who does not provide for their relatives, and especially for their own household, has denied the faith and is worse than an unbeliever." **1 Timothy 5:8**

"Blessings are Tied to the Family"

"Money doesn't change men it merely unmasks them. If a man is naturally selfish or arrogant or greedy, the money brings that out, that's all." **~Henry Ford**

"You've got to tell your money what to do or it will leave." **~Dave Ramsey**

"Money is only a tool. It will take you wherever you wish, but it will not replace you as the driver."
~Ayn Rand

"Parents who want less entitled kids have to be less entitled themselves." **~Kristen Welch**

"Children are not a distraction from more important work. They are the most important work."
~C.S. Lewis

"Humility is not thinking less of yourself it's thinking of yourself less." **~C.S. Lewis**

"Selflessness is humility. Humility and freedom go hand in hand. Only a humble person can be free."
~Jeff Wilson

"If you make money your god, it will plague you like the devil." **~Henry Fielding**

> Every man has 2 men in him ~ A King and a Fool. How do you know when you've found a queen? When she speaks to the King in you ~**Dr. Mike Murdock** ...

I have always tried to honor and respect the members and culture of the United States Armed Forces. Several of my family members served in the armed forces and represented our family, community, state, and country with distinction. My grandfather served in World War II, my Father served in Vietnam, and many of my uncles served in different branches of the military including the United States Army, Navy, and Air Force. What I respect most about the United States Military system is the discipline, rank structure, protocols, uniforms and camaraderie created and developed by physical, mental, and emotional training. Of all the military training types, people often only get to see, in real-time, coordinated physical fitness training (PT), which is usually introduced during Basic Training. Soldiers line up in ranks and after prompting from their drill sergeants, begin to walk or run in a coordinated fashion to a military cadence Vocal Syncopated Military Music (VSMM).

> "A Military cadence is a traditional call that is used as a song during running and marching formations to help keep soldiers in-step. Cadences are used to instill

> teamwork, build camaraderie and to boost the morale of a unit. Cadence commands such as "left foot, right foot" keep the platoon synchronized while in a running formation. A military cadence is also used to motivate and inspire military personnel to push through fatigue" (Marlatt, 2020).
>
> "The two primary types of cadence calls are the marching cadences at 120 beats per minute and running cadences which move at 10 beats per minute" (History of Military Cadences, 2014).

I am now entering Year 5 of my Blended Family Basic Training experience. Things have gotten better, but I am still trying to figure out several complex things. Every day seems to bring on new physical, spiritual, emotional, and financial challenges, but I am up for the task. I still show up for "Family Business" every day, try to listen and learn more attentively now, and work to quickly recognize verbal and non-verbal communication queues from my family drill instructors. The goal is to gain knowledge, get understanding, and get things right. Thankfully, I am not a Private E-2 anymore, but I am also not the Sergeant Major of this blended family. I am motivated to work harder to find the resources ($$) to become a much better provider. As I think about it now, I wonder what my motivating military cadence/ chant is that keeps me in step while I am running and marching to be a better STEPFATHER/STEPDADDY. It would probably sound something like the following and be led in a Call and Response Pattern by a drill sergeant that sounds like **Lou Rawls**, **Howlin Wolf**, and **Coach Pain** combined.

Step Daddy Marching/Running Cadence (Slow Pace Version)

I Say Your Left! Left! Left! Right! Left! (Master Sergeant)-Repeat[4X]

I Don't Know What You've Been Told- **Master Sergeant**
I Don't Know What You've Been Told- **Specialist Rice**
MAN Is King But Woman Is Gold!- Master Sergeant
MAN Is King But Woman Is Gold!- Specialist Rice
Leave Your Feelings At The Door!- Master Sergeant
Leave Your Feelings At The Door!- Specialist Rice
Selfish Ways Will Work No More!- Master Sergeant
Selfish Ways Will Work No More!- Specialist Rice
Make Your Money While You Can!- Master Sergeant
Make Your Money While You Can!- Specialist Rice
Pay Your Tithes And Make Big Plans!- Master Sergeant
Pay Your Tithes And Make Big Plans!- Specialist Rice
You Provide And They Will Spend!- Master Sergeant
You Provide And They Will Spend!- Specialist Rice
Do Your Job The Family Will Win!- Master Sergeant
Do Your Job The Family Will Win!- Specialist Rice
Morning, Noon Through Day and Night!- Master Sergeant
Morning, Noon Through Day and Night!- Specialist Rice
Be Encouraged It's Alright!- Master Sergeant
Be Encouraged It's Alright!- Specialist Rice

This Is Hard But That's OK!- Master Sergeant
This Is Hard But That's OK!- Specialist Rice
Strong MEN Take It Anyway!- Master Sergeant
Strong MEN Take It Anyway!- Specialist Rice
Honor, Family Is Your Code!- Master Sergeant
Honor, Family Is Your Code!- Specialist Rice
See What Will The Future Hold!- Master Sergeant
See What Will The Future Hold!- Specialist Rice
Don't Get Weary And Don't Quit!- Master Sergeant
Don't Get Weary And Don't Quit!- Specialist Rice
Trust In God And Spiritual Gifts!- Master Sergeant
Trust In God And Spiritual Gifts!- Specialist Rice
Maybe Get Your Thanks One Day!- Master Sergeant
Maybe Get Your Thanks One Day!- Specialist Rice
Thank YOU, Good Jobs Are Delayed!- Master Sergeant
Thank YOU, Good Jobs Are Delayed!- Specialist Rice
This Will Be Your Strongest Test!- Master Sergeant
This Will Be Your Strongest Test!- Specialist Rice
Complete This Work And God Will Bless!- Master Sergeant
Complete This Work And God Will Bless!- Specialist Rice
Hold Your Head Up Really High!- Master Sergeant
Hold Your Head Up Really High!- Specialist Rice
See Your Efforts Far And Wide!- Master Sergeant
See Your Efforts Far And Wide!- Specialist Rice
Dig In Deeper Never Doubt!- Master Sergeant
Dig In Deeper Never Doubt!- Specialist Rice
Step Daddy's Show Up & Show Out!- Master Sergeant
Step Daddy's Show Up & Show Out!- Specialist Rice
I Say Your Left! Left! Left! Right! Left! (Master Sergeant

> Halt! At Ease Soldier! Good Job!
> Report Tomorrow at 0800
> For this Continually Hard, Meaningful, and Godly Work! Dismissed!

I have made adjustments to my attitude, emotional nature, and focus for the family. The easiest thing for me to do was to pick up the pace to my providing, which meant working and trying to save more money. This was a task as all the funds that came in from multiple jobs left just as quickly. It was cool because working with the goal to get paid was right in my wheelhouse. It was easy for me to focus on earning more money because I could see an immediate impact in the family. I needed more emotional and psychological wins in that area, but a strange thing started happening to me. I was now in StepDaddy/Daddy Mode that began somewhere between Year 4 and the beginning of Year 5. My financial priorities changed. When I shopped, I found myself only thinking about the needs and wants of the family. I had pulled myself out of the equation and learned how to shop and spend money with a plan and purpose for my Wife, children, and on rare occasions my Mother-in-law.

I have never been a "cheap" person, and my LEO personality only supports the purchase and possession of the "finer things in life," not only for me, but also for others. I was different in a sense because when I finally recovered from the initial financial rollercoasters, early in my blended family experience, with a hope that I would catch up on material things I missed out on, I could only think about the needs of the family. I was not burdened with that responsibility, but was still motivated to provide. One of the issues that came up for me was to better budget the money that I made to make the biggest impact. I had bills, my Wife, had bills, and the children had bills, for which I was responsible. As an assistant professor, I had a stable job, but did not make a lot of money.

My second evening job was helpful financially, but put more pressure on me, raised my blood pressure, and through stress and late-night eating, caused me to gain more weight. I also had to do some financial maneuvering each year to prepare for the summer months since my appointment ended each year in May. I had to find money where I could, borrow it, or let some bills go. I decided that I was going to focus on the bills of the family and play (Hide-&-Seek) with my bills, but paid all of the other bills on time. My efforts were admirable, but all that did was cause everyone around me to have "Good Credit" and me to have "Bad Credit." I was OK with that because my family was 1st for me now, and if I had to take some financial Ls, I would take them with PRIDE to make sure that the family had what they needed. There was probably a better way to do that or find a balance so that my credit score did not take the biggest hit, but there was not enough money to go around.

I finally found a balance, and got things under control. I shared my resources equally with my Wife and the family, even if it put ME in a bind. I had gone from one extreme to the other because I wanted to see immediate results. One of the reasons why many Blended Families do not last is because people in these units often blend DEBT sometimes created from previous relationships and circumstances, financial missteps, student loans, unpaid collections, child support, and overdue medical bills. These are major challenges which people really need to discuss and understand before blending families. Then one day the subject of "Tithing" came up at a time that I really did not want to hear it. As a boy, every Sunday in church, a Deacon would stand before the congregation and typically say:

> "Bring ye all the tithes into the storehouse, that there may be meat in mine house, and prove me now herewith, saith the LORD of hosts, if I will not open you the windows of heaven, and pour you out a blessing, that there shall not be room enough to receive it."
>
> **Malachi 3:10**

This was the motivation to give to the church as clearly outlined in the Bible.

> "Honor the Lord with your wealth and with the first fruits of all your produce; then your barns will be filled with plenty, and your vats will be bursting with wine."
>
> **Proverbs 3:9-10.**

Throughout my adult life, there were times when I was disciplined enough to "Tithe" a little and other times when I wanted to "Tithe" a lot, which is funny because 10% is still 10% no matter how you look at it. My math was probably bad, and I began mixing offerings with tithes, which are different, but **YOU** get what I am saying. My answer to Tithing was no, because all of the funds and resources were needed to go toward bills first, and them when those got paid, then I would begin Tithing again. I developed a "No Tithing Logical-Mathematical mindset," as if I had negotiated with God. I "reconciled," which was one of my Mother's favorite words, while "Reprobate Mind, was one of my Father's favorite phrases. However, in my mind, God would understand that I needed my money to go toward bills, instead of the church. I was completely firm in that belief because I could not see or understand how taking more money away from bills would help me in the short and long-term. It was in the Bible, but as a STEPDADDY/STEPFATHER, all I understood was that bill numbers increased month-to-month, but my paychecks stayed the same. Not to mention that I would get nervous in February, of each year, because I knew my main job paychecks would stop in four months. Summer work was never guaranteed, so I was scrapping to make my money stretch. I was the "Provider" of this blended family, so that was my responsibility. (I think **YOU** know why I emphasized Provider, wait for it). I did feel a little guilty, from time to time, but felt that God would understand because He knows what I am going through. Tithing never came up formally until Year 5, but I know I did not Tithe consistently through Years 1-4. If I did not Tithe then, I "Sho" was not going to

Tithe now." I just kept praying and asking God for extensions on those Tithes like I did with the electric, gas, cable, water, mortgage, student loans, insurance, and car notes. I also tried to keep a tab on missed Tithes in my mind, with the goal to catch up eventually.

My pastor made a plea for members of the church to improve their Tithing and Giving, but I was not committed. My Wife made a plea for me to improve my Tithing knowing that I was already struggling with three sets of bills, and still not committed. I had to figure this money situation out on my own, without Tithing, because that just did not make any sense to me. What happened next was amazing! My hours were reduced on my second evening job and the summer school teaching opportunity in STEM usually offered to me in the Biology department, was given to someone else. Why? I needed that money. Stress! Stress! Stress! I am the Provider. This was a bad look for me and I need a "Victory."

As I contemplated my next move on how this financial puzzle would be solved, I began to understand and realize that old saying "less can be more." I was out of options and my finances were tight. I decided to "quietly" reinstate Tithing by ignoring required payment on a few of my other bills. My credit was "Super Bad" by now, so it really did not matter. The bill collectors kept calling, late fees were still accruing, and I still felt a sense of helplessness in controlling my family's debt. I was still looking for instant results and praying for a breakthrough, as if when I placed the envelope in the collection tray my bills would disappear. That did not happen, but something else did. As hard as it was for me to secure a Tithe from each one of my paychecks, I did it and things slowly changed.

I was still in debt, but I noticed that I had more wisdom to negotiate repayment terms. Suddenly the words through the phone and in my letters, were more thoughtful and on point. It was as if a mental fog was lifted that helped me to address past due accounts more strategically. Instead of paying more than I could afford, to try to "impress," past due bill account holders, and (still getting a negative indicator on my credit report each month), I paid less, which made things more manageable for me over time and allowed me to Tithe. I had developed a new spirit to the Tithe, but was still looking for the major financial breakthrough. As my Tithing increased, I began to see and feel God's Grace & Mercy in the major aspects of my blended family life. New job opportunities opened up to help with some of the "lack" I was experiencing as a 9-month employee. Some of my co-workers would often ask why I did not spread my salary over 12-months to make sure I would have money during the summers.

My answer was very simple: Stretching my resources over 12-months, meant that I would have less money each month to spend, so I would struggle for 9-months to make ends meet and then during the summer, I still struggled because I could not save during that period. My point is that when I committed to Tithing things did change for me for the better. As my pastor would say "I am just talking about what I'm talking about," so, **YOU** have to make the best decision for **YOU**, but I am convinced that when I finally decided to commit to Tithing, my financial portfolio changed.

Things got better and the true Provider, God Almighty, opened up more blessings. I was still in high debt with bad credit, like most people, but I was not as stressed as I was in the past. New work opportunities and Favor, helped me to get the additional resources which changed my life for the better. I still had a greater responsibility to continue to give above and beyond, as I received, realizing that my situation could have been worse. My Aunt Dorothy, my Mother's sister, tells me often "If **YOU** give, **YOU** will never be broke." I tried it, not just at my church, but freely giving of my time (volunteering), educational resources, knowledge, and enthusiasm for helping and assisting others at the University and in the greater community. Nevertheless, I began to appreciate Aunt Dorothy's advice even more.

I was rolling now as Blessings gave me an opportunity to not live life so "Close to the Ground," as my Father would say. Funds were coming in, and now it was time to spend some of those resources on me. Something else amazing happened! Every time I got a Blessing above and beyond what I worked for or expected and made plans to spend those funds on me, somebody in the family would need something. Like clockwork, as Financial Blessings came in, needs would arise to the point that I began to question if what I was experiencing was real. I had taught myself to be disciplined with money in a way that motivated me to always direct it to a core family need without pause, but the Blessings and need patterns started to be more than a coincidence.

Every time I received a Blessing, without fail, serious family business needs arose. I didn't know how to feel about that since I was receiving the blessings, but I had to use them for things other than myself. Things had turned around for me, so I was conflicted and didn't want to be ungrateful, but at the same time wondered when some of these wonderful financial blessings would stay with me. That is when I realized that "Blessings are Tied to My Family." As a soldier trying to join the *Army of the Lord*, I was the leader, head, and channel for the blessings. Several WOMEN in my church explained to me, early in my marriage, that a MAN/Husband/StepFather/Father is always judged by the appearance and demeanor of his Wife and children.

The Family Provider Unwritten Rules dictate that it is the husband's responsibility to maintain the structure, comfort, order, and success of the family, which is often tied to "How does his wife's hair look?" "What kind of car does she drive as compared to his?" "Does he burden his wife with his family responsibilities? "Does he run from his responsibilities to his wife or children?" "Is he a faith leader in the family?" "Does he know how to apologize when he believes or knows he is right?"- Rev. Robert L. Handley. "Can he take Ls for the health and wellbeing of the family? I thought about all of these questions, as I pondered what to do when I received a check blessing in the mail. No one knew about this magnificent $3,000 Check Blessing but me, so I was "conflicted" as to whether I should keep it to myself and finally get those items I had waited years to be able to afford or share this Blessing with the family.

As I was about to ATM deposit that check, take my Tithes off the top in three crisp $100 bills, and then head right to *Dillard's, JCPenney, Academy Sports, Best Buy, Lowe's, Home Depot, Walmart, Verizon, Red Lobster, and Big Banjo Pizza*, I thought about it. "This is a Test! This is only a Test! Of The Emergency Blessing System!" I had already seen the pattern of Blessings that were designed to pay unknown bills, but this time nothing was pressing, so I thought I was in the clear, but I did not want to wait until I was not. I paused for a moment, said "Thank You Lord!" and then drove off without depositing the check.

I went home and waited for something to happen. The next day people started having mouth pain, and we received a collection notice for a past due medical bill, from three years ago, that no one knew anything about. I realized then that "All of my Blessings are Tied to My Family. Without my family, there would be no need for God to Bless me over and above what I need, not want. My financial success was tied to my family's success, which was also tied to my success as the Family's MAN/Husband/StepFather/Father. I am glad I waited to cash that check and then go on a 3-hour shopping spree. Truth be told, I understand a little bit about how God works. I am sure if I tried to cash that check, something would have happened to prevent that since my intentions were not aligned with God's plan (Lesson Learned (LLs).

YEAR 6

> "Love is patient, love is kind. It does not envy, it does not boast, it is not proud. It does not dishonor others, it is not self-seeking, it is not easily angered, it keeps no record of wrongs." **1 Corinthians 13:4-5**

"It's Not Personal! She Loves The Children More Than You!"

Love: [luv]- n.
1. an intense affection for another person based on personal or familial ties 2. the deep tenderness, affection, and concern felt for a person with whom one has a relationship.

Year 6 begins with me feeling pretty good about what I learned in Year 5, regarding my role as Step Daddy in this blended family. I was still in it and after I realized the value of the **Blended Family Boot Camp Training** things were settling down. Now, after being patient, I felt it was time to get back to what I "want" and more importantly "need" from everybody in this blended family. I dealt with, and embraced, being called "Mr. Sederick." I like titles and what I once thought was a slight, I now wear proudly as a badge of honor. I also recognized that family traditions were already in place before me. Further, I saw the true value and power of a Mother and Mother-in-law in a blended family, and understood that my job as earthly provider is to work hard and unselfishly make sure the family never lacks. I have gotten it done so now I need my "Love Bucket," filled to the rim with recognition, appreciation, better communication, and maximum emphasis on my Love Languages. What I did not realize, like many people, is that I expected someone else to fill my "Love Bucket" but that process is based on self-care and self-love. Big emphasis on "Self."

Before we get into Lessons Learned (LLs) from Year 6, let us take a moment to understand the **Types of Love**, as a backdrop to my experiences in this blended family. Six types of Love include *Eros*, which is a romantic, and passionate love is associated with physical beauty. *Ludus* is a game-playing or uncommitted love associated with lies and deceptions with no level of commitment. *Storage* is a slow developing friendship-based love that develops and supports long-term relationships. *Pragma* is a type of unromantic love that is practical in nature and mutually beneficial. *Mania* is an obsessive or possessive type of love that can be extreme and is often associated with jealousy. *Agape* is a rare all-giving love that is not concerned about self, but focuses on the needs and compassion for others (Types of Love, 2016).

Now back to me. The time had come for me to fill that "Love Bucket" while I was working, parenting, living, and close to figuring this blended family thing out. My expectations were very high and as usual I wasn't as patient and understanding as I should have been. *Competition* reared its ugly head again in my spirit and now I was competing for the love the children received. Don't get me wrong. I was very clear about what I needed, which was to always be acknowledged as right, listened to all the time, and experience a clear shift in the blended family love dynamic completely toward me and my needs. **(Feel Free to Laugh Loudly from a Healthy Place!)** (Wait! Are we here again?) Yep!

I felt my life has been on one of my favorite types of playground equipment, the See-Saw. Even as a boy, I would always enjoy the See-Saw because when playing, one side would always go up and the other side would always go down at the same time.

Illustration of my metaphorical Love and Need See-Saw adapted from (Stop Keeping Score, 2020)

I was at a point in my Blended Family Step Daddy life where I wanted the See-Saw tilted all the way to my side, while I left the other rider in the air (metaphorically). What I am really saying is that I wanted to feel that the Love distribution balance was more focused only on my Love Language needs. (Get It?) **YOU** may be wondering why I am, and have been, so detailed in describing things about my character and personality that often do not present me in a positive light. I continue to share personal and private things that make me appear unstable, sometimes childish, selfish, stubborn, and overly sensitive. I told **YOU**! That is the real point of this book. When **YOU** know better, **YOU** often do and get better. And to do and get better means, **YOU** have to be authentic, real, honest, fearless, courageous, and open about who **YOU** are as a person and accept a hard evaluation and assessment of your core strengths and weaknesses.

As a MAN and StepDaddy/Daddy in a blended family, it is extremely important that You take a hard look at yourself and **Identify** and **Recognize**, which are two different things, your **Insecurities, Fears, Impact of Unresolved Issues in Your Childhood or Adult Life, and Mental Health status.** If YOU address those things with prayer, self-reflection, counseling, and family and social support, **YOU** can't convince me that **YOU** will not be equipped to Step Up and Show Out!

Remember the positive and negative traits listed under "I AM A LEO" at the beginning of the book? (Pause here). Even the title of Year 6 is misleading to a certain extent "It's Not Personal! She Loves the Children More Than **YOU**" because as readers, **YOU** are now more familiar with the different types of Love and know that YOU can Love differently based on the "type" of relationship. Was the relationship between my Wife and the children different from mine? (Think About It!) The title of Year 6 was also an interpretation of how I was feeling at that time. How many times have I been right about the circumstances and situations in this blended family up until this point? How many times have **YOU** felt a certain way about something in a family, but were off base or just completely wrong? Think About It! I had to learn what was impacting my decision-making; **Intellect or Emotion**. Was I rationalizing emotionally as to why I needed "all the Love" available in the family during Year 6? Why didn't I give my Intellect priority to fight against that Lack of Love Self-Pity Overbearing Attitude?

Now let's get back to the story.

So now, it is all about the Love for "Mr. Sederick." As a parent with responsibilities to provide the family with what they need, **YOU** can imagine the mental rollercoasters and conundrums I was putting myself through (Personal Torment For No Reason). I was still trying to self-actualize and get to the top (Maslow's Hierarchy of Need Pyramid), but the people I think need to make that happen are depending on me to make that happen for them. I was unbalanced (See-Saw). I wanted to be selfish, but that was hard because I learned to enjoy giving so much. The MAN in me would not allow me to slight the family, for my own personal gains, or to make a point, but something had to give.

Why is everyone else getting what I feel I am missing? Do they know? "Do they care? I guess it was my fault because I really never said anything. I just expected people around me to read my mind and understand how I felt. Was that fair? Surely not, but it made sense to me in a way that supported a victimized persona. **YOU** have probably seen and/or experienced those scenarios before where "hurt" feelings lead to more attention. I wanted my non-verbal communication queues and body language to do the work for me. I describe this as "Telling **YOU** something, without telling **YOU**." I wanted the family to feel that something and see me behave as if something was wrong, but never said that something was wrong. How frustrating is that? To me, very! But when **YOU** are on the receiving end of new emphasis and focus, even though it was promoted by **YOU** being disingenuous and manipulative, it feels like a win. I was overusing my non-verbal communication skills before I knew what they were. A key word going forward is *Communication*. Now, let us discuss non-verbal communication styles. Did **YOU** know that **YOU** had non-verbal communication skills? Are **YOU** using those skills selflessly or selfishly? I have been waiting for a while to finally put those two adverbs together in the text.

Non-Verbal Communication

There are several non-verbal communication styles that people use conscientiously or sub-conscientiously to interact with people in their families, on their jobs, in public, and now across the Internet using social media and gaming technology platforms (FaceTime, Google Duo, Zoom, GoToMeeting, Skype, Cisco WebEx, YouTube, Twitch, etc.) Non-verbal communication (the way **YOU** listen, look, move, and react) is very important in any relationship and it impacts your ability to communicate well (Melinda, 2019) (Effective Communication, 2012). It is important that non-verbal communication matches the words spoken to build trust, clarity, and connection or tension, mistrust, and confusion could result (Melinda, 2019) (Effective Communication, 2012).

Non-verbal communication can play five major roles including **Repetition**, which repeats and strengthens the verbal message; **Contradiction** which contradicts your verbal message and causes your listener to believe you are speaking the truth; **Substitution** occurs when body language such as a facial expression tells a clearer story over words, **Complementing,** such as a form of praise, can increase the impact of a message, and **Accenting**, which can be a physical gesture, such as raising your voice or writing in all caps in a text message (Melinda, 2019) (Effective Communication, 2012).

Have **YOU** ever felt this way? Instead of saying what **YOU** really want or need to say or doing what you really want or need to do **YOU** rely only on non-verbal communication? That was me. I felt I had earned the right to be "complicated," so that my family would work hard to figure me out. This is a good spot where you can **(Feel Free to Laugh Loudly from a Healthy Place)**.

There are several types of nonverbal communications or body languages including: **Facial Expression (Classic)** provides emotions without words; **Body Movement and Posture** demonstrates how **YOU** perceive other people by your stance and movements; **Gestures** apply to people who speak with their hands, clapping for emphasis during a conversation, or making animated movements while speaking; **Eye Contact** can indicate interest, affection, hostility or attraction and helps the flow of conversation; **Touch** is associated with handshakes or hugs; **Space** "In one's personal space" can indicate affection, aggression, or dominance; and finally **Voice** (It's not what **YOU** say, It's how **YOU** say it!) loudness, timing, pace, tone, inflection, and words such as "Alrighty Then!" "Ahh!" "Uh-Huh!" "Whatever!" "Pa-lease!" and "Are you serious?" "can indicate sarcasm, anger, affection, or confidence" (Melinda, 2019) (Effective Communication, 2012). I am sure I used all of the non-verbal communication styles in Year 6, positively and negatively.

I am now going to set the stage for the major breakthroughs for me that came near the end of Year 6. As I watched my blended family dynamic unfold, there were times when I was so Needy that arguments would occur just for the sake of arguments. (Has this ever happened to **YOU**?) My non-verbal turned into verbal and then my verbal turned into misunderstandings, which led to more non-verbal to prompt verbal, which eventually led to more misunderstanding. The only thing I focused on was the need for the "Love Bucket" to be filled, but the question is with what? Did I know what I wanted? Could I tell my family what I needed? Is wanting "everything" too broad? Is feeling that way being unrealistic in my role as Step Daddy? I already knew that my Wife was very busy with three children, employed, and working on another degree, but hey "What about me?" I am here. Where was my understanding? I expected her to be Superwoman, but the Kryptonian symbol on my chest that was supposed to represent the "Man of Steel" (Goyer, 2013) was not glowing. Watch *Man of Steel* (Goyer, 2013) to get this reference. When **YOU** come to the part when Superman is about to take his first flight, as his Father's conscientiousness tells him "The only way YOU will know how strong YOU are is to keep testing your limits," should put everything **YOU** feel, believe, think, or know **YOU** are going through, on your blended family journey into perspective.

> Then, I had a revelation and instantly realized and spoke directly to my intrusive thoughts, low self-esteem, fears, insecurities, past, and needy nature, **"It is Not Personal! She Loves the Children More Than You!"**

YOU have been reading up to this point in the book, and probably thought that somewhere during Year 6, my Wife or Mother-in-law had to sit me down and say and/or explain this to me, but it was "I" who came to that realization. The ironic part is that is what I have always wanted in the first place. The value I see in any Mother, including my Mother, Wife, Mother-in-law, aunties, cousins, etc., is a different set of skills, strategies, approaches, and a profound level of patience for children and situations which are beyond my capabilities. I finally accepted it! There are gifts that my Wife and Mother-in-law have that I will never have, and I am OK with that. It became clear to me when a member of the family passed away, and my Wife explained the death to my daughter in a way that brought acknowledgement, understanding, and peace in the most simple, direct, and compassionate way. I was amazed that I did not know how to do that, but was so glad that there was a Mother, in the picture, with the physical, mental, emotional connection, experience, and Mother Wit to help a child understand the loss at a young age. That is why I kept saying to myself over, and over, and over again, "It is Not Personal! She Loves the Children More Than You!" I saw and experienced *Agape Love*, in that moment, and literally and figuratively stopped carrying around that empty "Love Bucket," and stopped waiting for a situation, scenario, or someone to fill it. Do **YOU** have a Love Bucket that needs to be filled? Are **YOU** prepared to enjoy a filled "Love Bucket," or will **YOU** still complain, pour out the contents and expect it to be filled again? (Think About It!)

Illustration of a Typical Love Bucket

As a side note, I Love writing because I can add little clues in the text to reveal things to the reader to try to get that Aha! Moment! Here is one. When you look at the title of this book: StepDads Showing Up & Showing Out: ***Tips for Navigating the <u>Complex World</u> of Blended Families***, did YOU know that the *Complex World* part of the title was referring to me? You probably thought that the complexities of my experiences as a StepFather/StepDaddy was related to what the other key players in the blended family (Wife, Mother-in-law, children, in-laws, etc.) did or did not do. Nope! Hopefully, now **YOU** realize that the *Complex World* is mine and I have to own the positivity and negativity associated with it. I wish I could wink at **YOU** with that "Get It?" (non-verbal communication vibe.) Wait! I can do that. ☺

What I realized in Year 6 was that in order to change my blended family experience, I had to finally change the Step Daddy in me "all the way." No one could put that work in for me, but me, which I believe was God's plan. I told **YOU** before that I often take double Ls (LLs) to get understanding and wisdom because I can be stubborn, hard-headed, egotistical, and pretentious. I wanted to do better, so I tapped into *Storage Love* and reached out to family members, friends, pastors, deacons, teachers, mentors, and church members to ask them for advice, hear their stories, and share my blended family living and learning experiences. I wanted and needed "Counseling," from members of a "Wise Counsel," to help me gain Tips for Navigating the *Complex World* of Blended Families.

YEAR 7

"Where there is strife, there is pride, but wisdom is found in those who take advice."-**Proverbs 13:10**

"Where there is no guidance, a people falls; but in an abundance of counselors there is safety."-**Proverbs 11:14**

"Wise Counsel!"

We are nearing the end of the book and by now **YOU** have learned a little more about my life and growth and development as a STEPFATHER/STEPDADDY. I have taken some time, in this part of the book, to recognize, honor, and say Thank You to the people who have helped me navigate this journey. This important group of "authentic" people includes family members, friends, teachers, mentors, co-workers, and church members who have watched, counseled me, and supported my journey as a STEPFATHER/STEPDADDY. Sometimes they just listened, as I complained about the struggles I was experiencing in a blended family. Other times, they provided good advice, did not accept my often one-sided view of things and then gave me clear guidance and strategies to help me make things work. I think the most effective strategies, some of the members of the "Wise Counsel" used to help me, were to watch me struggle to find the answers, listen to me as I asked them for answers to the puzzles controlling my circumstances, and then explain to me that I needed to figure it out on my own. That is Powerful! That is Deep! That is Love!

Members of the "Wise Counsel" are not listed in any particular order (alphabetical or otherwise) and are not ranked based on their importance or impact because each of them is equally important in helping me Show Up & Show Out as a STEPFATHER/STEPDADDY. I will still speak to some of their characteristics (humorously) as I highlight their greater role in my life. If **YOU** are a **MAN** (and the **WOMEN** who love and adore them) who is taking on the responsibility of a blended family, develop and appreciate a "Wise Counsel" to help **YOU**. It will make a BIG difference!

Dr. Reed

Thank You!

Thank You Dr. Reed, for still being a Father figure to me after more than 25 years. Your efforts so many years ago set that stage for me to earn a Ph.D. and now work at our Alma Mater. I appreciate your wisdom, patience, mentorship, attention to detail, work ethic, and desire to always open doors and opportunities for me. I never want to let you down, which has strengthened my professionalism, accountability, and passion for the important work in Higher Education. I also thank you for often "pulling me out of that emotional convoluted tree," and helping me to stay focused on tasks, without allowing my emotions to rule my intellect. God Bless!

Isaac "Ike"

Thank You!

Thank You "Ike" for supporting my growth and development as a MAN, Husband, Stepfather, Father, and Teacher. You provided a musical, philosophical, and family model for me to follow, when things got tough. Your words of encouragement, when I needed them the most, helped me to stay on the course and understand the importance of true commitment in a blended family, and how to keep working toward the ultimate goal of caring for those whom God put under my charge. Love You!

Greg "G-Money"

Thank You!

Thank You Greg (G-Money) for your wisdom, experience, mentoring, and culinary skills. I am still trying to learn how to cook the perfect "Liver & Onions." You taught me to continue to work hard and encouraged me to be a StepDaddy and resource for the family. You motivated me to always improve as a MAN. No one can "Product This like G-Money!" I benefitted from your advice, patience, listening ear, resources, life lessons, energy, and approach to living. Love You!

Wash

Thank You!

Thank You Wash for still being a wise mentor, friend, and colleague since the early 90s. I can still share my perspectives and experiences with you, as you can look back in my life as your former student and in my future as a professional. You have also helped me to think and understand how to navigate difficult situations, especially in my family. Your advice to "Turn Up Your Level of Kindness," to resolve conflicts at work and at home, was timely and helped me address challenges that continued to stress me out and distracted me from the plan God has for my life. Love You!

Josie

Thank You!

Thank You Josie for being a "Big Sister," mentor, friend, professional listener, writing coach, brainstormer, professional goal cheerleader, image consultant, counselor, psychologist, and encourager for the last 25 years. I appreciate your spirit, wisdom, experience, laughter, "woman's perspectives," and Mother Wit that have helped me to see things in my family and life differently. You have also helped me to understand that, "The way I see situations, is not always how they really are." Thank you for showing me how to "Fight Fire with Water, Not Fire!" Your wisdom and support over the years have supported my education, being featured in Ebony Magazine, and writing and publishing multiple books. God Bless!

The Locketts

Thank You!

Thank You to the Locketts for being good friends, supporters, and mentors. You have helped me to understand and deal with the "politics" of life, in the workplace, and the "ins and outs" of running for public office. I appreciate the opportunity to be able to share my ideas and frustrations with you, as you helped me continue to see the "Big Picture" and improve in several areas of my life. One of my biggest issues has always been "perspective," and how I needed to learn to see things with wide-angled lenses and not tunnel vision. I also value your commitment to each other for over 15 years, which provides me with another positive example to follow and model. God Bless!

Omie

Thank You!

Thank You Omie for providing a Mother's perspective to help me understand that even though I might mean well and want to do and be all things magnificent as somebody's StepFather/StepDaddy, I had to understand the strong bond and relationship between a Mother, her children, and all the things that happened before I came into the picture. Our conversations on the church van helped me to recognize that my oftentimes aggressive take-charge bossy nature, may work in some situations, but not in all. Especially, as it relates to my interactions with my Wife and children. You helped to remind me of one of the golden rules. "Pick and choose your family battles carefully because all of them are not worth the effort or the fight!" God Bless!

The Fishers

Thank You!

Thank You to the Fishers for your Love, guidance, support, and care over the years. I appreciate your financial help, mentoring, and wisdom, which helped me to rebuild my credit and create new streams of income to support my family. You are special because you still care about me and my family and still stay in touch, after all these years. I have learned so much from you over the years and I hope to continue to gain from your experiences. Your commitment to each other for over 26 years provides a good example for me to model. Through good times and bad times, you always have my back. Love You!

The Spears

Thank You!

Thank You to The Spears for being a part of my greater family, and always being open to hearing and understanding my perspectives, frustrations, and triumphs as a Husband, Father/Stepfather, worker, and provider. You are role models to me and my family because you always "Keep God First," work hard, have a strong and sustained loving partnership for more than 25 years, and continue to grow together as a unit spiritually, emotionally, and financially. Thank You for the opportunity to work in your business to earn money to pay a bill. It was the longest workday I ever experienced, but the financial Blessing, as a result, made a big difference. Love You!

Uncle C

Thank You!

Thank You Uncle C for always being yourself and never compromising your "core" beliefs. I thank you for your wisdom, experience, and ability to continue to challenge me not to be illogical in my approach to professional work relationships, marriage, and "family business." When you asked me "If I ask **YOU** to make me a dish, could **YOU** do it?" "I said Yes!" Then you asked me "If I ask **YOU** to make a dish that I like could YOU do it?" That simple wordplay exercise helped me to understand that if given the option, people can always find flaws in what **YOU** do or say, so there is no need to be overly concerned about what other people think. I also learned not to mess with anyone or anything that has "unlimited resources." Love You!

Rev. Dr. Robert and Carrie Handley

Thank You!

Thank You to Rev. Dr. Robert and Carrie Handley for your ministry, teaching, leadership, support, caring, strength, wisdom, and compassion for me, my family, and the families of others in our church. You are role models, wise counselors, and living examples for your more than 50 years of marriage and over 40 years in ministry. Your support for me and my family is appreciated and will never be forgotten. I hope to continue to support your ministry and family. Thank You Rev. Handley for your confidence and training to become one of your Deacons, and to understand that Godly Work is about Service. God Bless!

Donna

Thank You!

Thank You Donna for being a mentor, friend, and supporter of my professional and political aspirations. I truly thank you for helping me to understand the special relationship between a Mother and Son and how that bond is like no other. I thought I could just "jump in between that" as Husband, Father, Stepfather, MAN, and Provider. You helped me to understand the powerful role of a Mother in the lives of her children, to stop taking things personally regarding that bond, and to understand that whether I was in the picture or not, a Mother's first priority will always be her children. No matter how old they are! God Bless!

Aunt Marilyn

Thank You!

Thank You Aunt Marilyn for taking care of me when I was 1 year old and for still taking care of me now. I appreciate your efforts when Daddy was in the hospital. You led that effort. I am so thankful for your spirit, personality, support, and Love. I really appreciate your help in convincing my Father (your brother) to finally co-sign for me to borrow that $5,000. He would not listen to me, but he did listen to you, and you helped me negotiate. I was able to get that (loan) money and it changed my life. Love You!

Elder Karl and Lady Rochelle Barnes

Thank You!

Thank You Elder Karl and Lady Rochelle Barnes for your Love, support, ministry and wisdom as shepherds of the Gospel. I thank you for developing a space and atmosphere, where members of my family can worship and grow in the Word of God. When I did not understand my greater role in my family, you prayed for me, counseled me, helped me learn patience and understanding, and then instead of giving me the answers to the hard family questions, allowed me to figure things out on my own. Your commitment to each other for more than 48 years is a wonderful example for my family and me. God Bless!

Uncle Randall

Thank You!

Thank You Uncle Randall for being a mentor and wise teacher who helped me to understand how to operate in my blended family. As a family male role model, you helped me to understand my greater purpose and role in the family as Husband, Father, Stepfather, and Provider. Some questions you answered, while others you left for me to ponder and solve. I learned that the success of my family is directly tied to my work ethic, sacrifice, and ability to understand that my role is about service for the greater good of my family. Love You!

Deacon and Mother Hannah

Thank You!

Thank You Deacon (PawPaw) and Mother Hannah (Grannie) for your commitment to each other for more than 68 years. Thank You Deacon Hannah, for sparking a fire in me to be more committed to the work of the Lord in my church, as much as I was committed to my job. I will never forget when you asked me "How many times have you missed work? "I said none." Then, you explained to me that as a MAN, that level of effort and commitment is needed in my church. Your efforts put me on a path to become an ordained Deacon. I thank you Mother Hannah for your wisdom, Mother Wit, and caring for all the members of my family and your Love and support for Deacon Hannah. Love You!

Wayne & Penny

Thank You!

Thank You Wayne and Penny for your work, ministry, and family example in our church. Through your efforts, I have been able to sing and travel with the church choir, participate in Christmas and Easter programs, Black History Month Trivia, and support Church Anniversaries. You are also supportive as I work to be a better MAN and grow stronger in Christ. You have also been role models for my family and me, for 35 years of commitment to each other. Your Music and Youth Ministry leadership has also helped me to learn to be more patient, organized, diligent, and focused with the work I do in my family. God Bless!

Rev. Bernard and Anita Coleman

Thank You!

Thank You Rev. Bernard and Anita Coleman for your outreach and ministry, which motivated me to join and want to participate in church activities. I remember the day I came to church to worship, where my Mother did, before her passing. Before I left service, with the intention to maybe come back again, you reached out to me and invited me to come back. I agreed and your Evangelism connected me with a supportive and loving church family that has been a Blessing to my family and me since that time. Your family model and commitment to each other, for over 22 years, has also been a Blessing and a model for me to follow. God Bless!

Rev. Mike and Damiccah Robertson

Thank You!

Thank You Rev. Mike and Damiccah Robertson for your ministry and commitment to helping others raise God-fearing children. ***God's Planned Parenthood: What God Says About Raising Our Children*** is a great guide for me to reference when facing challenges. I also refer to that book to help me understand what God expects from me, as a MAN, in my family. I also thank you for demonstrating and providing insight and advice on how a Father, Mother, and Children can live, grow, operate, coexist and be successful as a Godly Unit. God Bless!

Kevin

Thank You!

Thank You "My Brother!" for being "My Brother." You have always been a good friend, mentor, confidant, and coach who challenged my understanding, views, and beliefs. You helped me to learn to slow down and not to be impulsive, emotionally extreme, naïve, and overly sensitive, as a leader at work, or in my family. I appreciate the Love, financial and emotional support that you and your family have shared with me over the years. I can always count on you. You also showed me that it is OK to expect and to get more out of life. I feel "I deserve good things too" and learned to expect good things for my family and me. Love You!

The Swifts

Thank You!

Thank You to The Swifts for your hospitality and allowing me to share my frustrations, fears, misunderstandings, and sometimes misplaced perceptions regarding "experiences in my family." I appreciate your Love, Afro-centric views and care for me, which helped redirect my negative thoughts into positive mindsets. I really appreciate the fact that when I tried to ignore things about myself, that made me uncomfortable, you helped me to address those things for my benefit. Ever since you shared with me the phrase, *"I Am Because We Are!"* it has become a theme of my life and work. I truly recognize the value and impact of mentoring from you both as my Elders. Love You!

Aunt Dorothy & Aunt Brenda

Thank You!

Thank You Aunt Dorothy & Aunt Brenda for always checking on me and keeping me connected to my Mother. I am glad I have an opportunity to spend time and help you with errands, just as my Mother did. When you remind me of the "Power of Charity," and say to me over and over again, "If you give, you will never be broke!" I took that to heart. I hope to continue to make you both proud of me. Please stop trying to pay me for the things I do as your "favorite" nephew. I could say more about how you also have taught me a "new level of patience," when we run errands and pay bills together, but I'll leave it right there. Love You!

The Cooleys

Thank You!

Thank You to The Cooleys for being down to earth people whom I can talk to about anything. "I Love The Cooleys" because I can be myself and share my pain, fears, shortcomings, and hopes for breakthroughs and real success, as I navigate through situations in my family. As manic as I can be at times, you both always stay calm in the midst of chaos, live life to the fullest, and whenever we get together, we laugh, brainstorm, figure things out, and solve the important problems. No matter what or how I am feeling, you support me. God Bless!

Mrs. Landers

Thank You!

Thank You Mrs. Landers for providing me with Mother Wit and for laughing with me at work. You help me to understand, as "panicked" as I can be at times about a financial situation (check), that sometimes it is "really not that serious and things will work out." I appreciate you providing an opportunity for me to talk and learn from you, on those days when things do not make sense. The most important lesson you helped me to learn is that sometimes, as a MAN, I have to take an L if that will help others feel better, or fix a major problem. Those experiences helped me to take more Ls in my family and on the job, but still be productive. God Bless!

The Hortons

Thank You!

Thank You to The Hortons for your hospitality and willingness to share your home with me. I also thank you for all those times when all I needed to do was "talk it out." You listened and gave me supportive advice without judging. You represent success and growth in marriage for me, as I have watched and learned from your relationship and family interactions, over the last 15 years. You also helped me to see both perspectives in a marriage and family and how children and extended family members support, lift, and seal that bond. "I Love the Hortons." God Bless!

Mrs. Faucette

Thank You!

Thank You Mrs. Faucette for your kindness, understanding, patience, and Mother Wit. I can always share my family experiences with you, because you understand and can see things from both sides of the situation. I trust your advice, criticisms, and honesty as a Son trusts and relies on his Mother for wisdom. We can be serious or laugh about how I think I should feel, but always recognize and understand the phrase "It is what it is." I truly appreciate your spirit and openness at work, which makes dealing with challenges at work a lot easier. God Bless!

Ralph

Thank You!

Thank You Ralph for just being you. You are great friend and mentor, since our high school days, and are a constant reminder of the power of brotherhood. I appreciate your listening ear and political, social, and educational perspectives, which have helped me to think and evaluate my goals and objectives more clearly. We fight like brothers, find common ground like brothers, and we Love and Respect each other like brothers! Your greatest talent in my life is helping me to separate Facts from Fiction so that I accept and learn, even if I do not want to. Love You Brother!

The Wards

Thank You!

Thank You to The Wards for your influence and support in my life. Your wisdom, experience, drive, and connection to each other motivate me in my family life. We have known each other for a long time and over the years our relationship has evolved. What still stays the same is my respect and appreciation for your resilience in marriage and in life and your 28 years of commitment to each other. For me, it is always good to see in others where I hope to be one day. You also represent a key example of the power of faith, perseverance, energy, and how things get better in marriage over time. God Bless!

Mrs. Baker

Thank You!

Thank You Mrs. Baker for helping me to refocus my efforts at work and begin to understand that my Blessings Are Tied To My Family. My ambition and drive to succeed and to be the provider, often caused me to forget that "Promotion Comes from the Lord." Your words of support and instruction also challenged me to use a Christian approach, compassion, and patience with people.

You also helped me see my family challenges in a new perspective, by sharing your experiences, which helped me to address my "not-listening," one-track approach to solving problems. Thank you for being a voice of reason, when I needed to hear some good advice and the truth. God Bless!

The Richardsons

Thank You!

Thank You to the Richardsons for being a wonderful example of how hard work and Committed Love sustains a family. I have seen your planning, patience, and work with your children and grandchildren and recognize your positive and sustained impact in their lives. I have learned from your interactions as husband and wife, work in the church, and outlook on life. Your 30-year commitment to each other is a lasting example to me and my family to know that the best is still yet to come. God Bless!

YEAR 8

> "So do not fear, for I am with you; do not be dismayed, for I am your God. I will strengthen you and help you; I will uphold you with my righteous right hand."
>
> Isaiah 41:10

"God is with YOU! Pray, Work, Listen, Watch, and Learn!"

Year 8 began for me with reconciliation, personal revelation, and daily reflection. I felt I had come full circle regarding my feelings, needs, wants, and insecurities about being a StepFather/StepDaddy. I was a lot more focused and learned to go back to my educational roots, but this time I leaned more heavily on God's Word. I was still referencing information in Dare To Be A Man (2010), by David G. Evans and used some of the chapter headings and quotes for motivation as a series of Dares or Challenges designed for improvement. **Dare To Be a Man of Vision**, "God has uniquely equipped you as a MAN to dramatically affect your surroundings and personally impact the people to whom you relate" (Evans, 2010). I realized that I was making a difference by my presence and effort and I am just not a patient person and wanted instant gratification and results. **Dare To Lead**, "The strength and integrity of your leadership ability is more profoundly revealed when you are faced with personal crisis" (Evans, 2010).

I know I was challenged from the very start of my blended family experience, while trying to figure things out as they happened, which sounds philosophical and deep to me, but reflects common sense for others. **Dare to Submit**, "Mutual submission invites into the relationship love, respect, honor, and dignity" (Evans, 2010). Throughout this experience, I thought the people in my blended family were supposed to submit to my will, follow my vision, and build me up as the leader. I learned that my submission was key to learning the ins and outs of my blended family experience, building relationships, and receiving the blessings and help from God and the people He placed in my life. I was told once that "It does not make **YOU** as a MAN, any weaker or stronger to be flexible, apologize, take an L for the team, or admit that **YOU** are wrong and need help." This was a profound lesson for me. Why did I have to be so BIG, when GOD was in control. **Dare to Forgive**, "The leadership a MAN brings to those he loves must always be tempered with mercy and grace" (Evans, 2010). I had to change my perspective by understanding the perspectives of my Wife, the children, and my Mother-in-law. I was operating under an **Agenda vs. Assignment** model. I felt I had an Assignment, and I wanted to earn an "A," but worried that an Agenda was already in place to prevent that. To be different, I had to think differently, and it took me a long time to trust the process, work the assignment, and know that the only Agenda was my steadfast work and contributions to the success of this blended family unit. Finally, **Dare to Praise**, "Most MEN understand military principles and terminologies- soldiers, combat, front lines, victory, and defeat, but when Biblical principles of military warfare are considered your understanding of the spiritual, will change dramatically" (Evans, 2010).

I began to see how God was granting me favor, understanding, opportunity, perfect timing for blessings, and setting the stage for me to stay the course and work my blended family assignment. I stopped thinking about my Assignment, as if I had a list of things to do and once I did those things, I was done. In reality, I tried to check off things, during the process, but as one challenge was overcome, others quickly developed. I then began to look for, prepare, and brace myself for future physical, emotional, psychological and financial challenges that would arise. As a MAN, I learned in the words of Anthony "Spice" Adams' alter ego, Cream

Biggums' quote to **"Stay Ready, So You Don't Have To Get Ready!"**

My church and church family also provided important support for me during Year 8. As a church body, our pastor led our study of Spiritual Gifts, also defined as "Something God has chosen specifically for a person to help with the advancement of the church, by serving and using a special ability" (Your Spiritual Gifts, 2020). The goal was to understand what one's gifts and talents are in ministry and how to best use those talents in a church, on a job, or in your family. Over the years, I learned that many of my successes occurred in areas of teaching, mentoring, and giving, but as a church, we dug deeper to discover the spiritual gifts of our members to understand where their talents would be best served. The goal was to support our church mission **"To Know Jesus Christ Better, and To Make Jesus Christ Better Known."**

> "As every man hath received the gift, even so minister the same one to another, as good stewards of the manifold grace of God." **1 Peter 4:10**

Spiritual Gifts

The nine spiritual gifts include **Evangelism, Prophecy, Teaching, Exhortation, Shepherding, Mercy-Showing, Serving, Giving,** and **Administration** (Church Growth. org, 2020). There may be some debate, from Bible Scholars, on number of spiritual gifts, based on **I Corinthians 12:1-11**, but the point is that I had an opportunity to look more closely, at my own spiritual gifts, which is foundational to my ability to succeed in a blended family. I took the test and my Top 3 Spiritual Gifts, based on the answers I provided, were **Serving**, **Shepherding**, and **Mercy-Showing** (Spiritual Gifts, 2018). As a Server, I wanted to do anything I could to support the church, as well as members of my family, and coworkers. My Shepherding Gift provided a capacity for me to lead training and caring for the needs of a group of Christians (Spiritual Gifts, 2018) or the faculty, staff, and students with whom I came into contact with daily. The Mercy-Showing Spiritual Gift allowed me to deal with and minister with people at church, at home, or at work, who would often be dealing with uncomfortable subjects and circumstances and needed someone to listen, encourage, and counsel. I also scored high in areas of Teaching, Exhortation, Administration, and Giving which meant that just like I have Multiple Intelligences, I have also been blessed with Multiple Spiritual Gifts which God can use for His Glory.

Now, I was an active Deacon, driving the church van, singing in the church choir (tenor), attending Sunday School and learning in **Men's Class #10**. When it was my time to bring the lesson highlights, I wanted to make sure I was on point. My pastor was a member of that class. As much as I thought I had understood about the lesson, I really wanted to hear from him and get his wisdom. Participating and learning in **Men's Class #10** also provided me with access to a community of older Christian MEN who had valuable knowledge and experience on many aspects of marriage, parenting, working, and living and succeeding in this life. Rev. Arnold E. Robertson, Jr., an Associate Minister at our church, wrote a book entitled ***God's Planned Parenthood: What God Says About Raising Our Children***. For me, this was another resource from which, I could benefit to be a better MAN in my blended family. In one chapter entitled "Is There a Man in the House?", there was one quote that stated, "As MEN, we must come to the realization that God created us, and He knows all about us. We often get to the point in our lives where we feel that we are MEN, and we don't need another MAN to tell us how to be MEN" (Robertson, 2016). I struggled with this because I did feel at one point that any advice or suggestions or knowledge from another MAN, was counterproductive to my desire to completely lead my blended family. Oh! How I was wrong! (Again!) The value of male family mentorship took me a long time to understand. I would sometimes think "If I listen or take advice from another MAN, that MAN would somehow be running my household?" "How can I listen to another MAN's family experience and believe it related to mine? My blended family is different!" These are just a few examples of how I was jaded and insecure about receiving Knowledge and Wisdom about things, that I really did not know anything about. (This is a typical response when someone is insecure about someone else knowing more about a subject than they do).

When I finally assessed the Wisdom in the room and recognized that some members of **Class #10** were married for over **20, 30, 40**, and even **50 years**, what else could I do but listen? It was time for me to sit at their table, break bread, and understand what could come next in my blended family

(Lesson Learned (LLs). Another quote from that same chapter stated "MEN, we cannot wait for society to take from us what we should give anyway. When we marry, our lives are no longer our own. When we assist in the creation of children, our lives end and theirs begin. We are to sacrifice for them such that they may have better lives, just as Christ did for us" (Robertson, 2016). This was powerful for me because I spent too many years looking for credit and praise for things I was supposed to be doing as Husband, Stepfather, Father, and earthly provider. As I pulled myself, and emotions out of things, I did, or tried to do for my blended family, I could feel the Confidence and Joy grow in my own Spirit, as God opened and closed more doors, I received more Favor, Protection, Opportunities, and Blessings. With the understanding that those things were not just for me, but primarily for the benefit of my family.

YEAR 9

> "Let us then approach the throne of grace with confidence, so that we may receive mercy and find grace to help us in our time of need." **Hebrews 4:16**

"If I Knew Then, What I Know Now? Lord! Thank You for Your Grace and Mercy!"

> When I was a child, I spake as a child, I understood as a child, I thought as a child; but when I became a man, I put away childish things. **I Corinthians 13:11**

> My son, despise not the chastening of the Lord; neither be weary of his correction for whom the Lord loveth he correcteth; even as a father the son in whom he delighteth. Happy is the man that findeth wisdom, and the man that getteth understanding. **Proverbs 3:11-13**

> Get wisdom, get understanding: forget it not; neither decline from the words of my mouth. Forsake her not, and she shall keep thee. Wisdom is the principal thing: therefore, get wisdom: and with all thy getting get understanding. **Proverbs 4:5-7**

Well, here we are in Year 9, and I am different and hope that **YOU** as a MAN, (and the WOMEN who love and adore him) are also in a different place of Love, Honor, and Respect for the family. One thing I hoped **YOU** noticed, as readers, is that the more I gained knowledge and understanding regarding my role in a blended family, the less I wrote. Year chapters are getting shorter and shorter as scriptures are speaking Truth to Power in my life and hopefully to the reader. This is by design because with greater discernment, I really have no reason to say more, just do more. It is truly amazing as to how far I have come since Year 1. **For the Bible Scholars, I am not trying to emulate The Shortest Book in the New Testament and Bible (KJV), which is?** (I'll give the answer at the end of this chapter.) I can now ask myself honestly and thoughtfully some tough questions regarding my mindset for work in a blended family and hope **YOU** do the same.

Blended Family Reflection Questions?

1) Was it All worth it? **YES!**
2) Am I A Better MAN for my Blended Family Experiences? **YES!**
3) Did this Blended Family Experience change me as a MAN? **YES!**
4) Are things in this Blended Family "exactly" (Be Careful) like I envisioned them? **There Is No Such Thing! That only means that there is more work for me and the family to do together.**
5) Am I ready to Quit? **No! Resting is OK, but Quitting is Not Allowed**
6) Did I GROW? **Absolutely!**
7) Do I have a Testimony for Others? **YES!**
8) Do I recommend this Experience for other MEN (and the WOMEN who love and adore them?) **(YES!), if YOU consider and think about some of the tips in Year 10**
9) Did I ever wonder Why Me? **YES! Until I realized that God presented the case, laid out the facts, and controls the outcome of the argument, Why Not Me! I'm "Mr. Sederick"**
10) Will there be StepDads Showing Up & Showing Out: Tips to Navigating the Complex World of Blended Families Part II? **YES!**

The Shortest Book in the New Testament and Bible (KJV) is:
3 John (200 words- Original Greek Language)

YEAR 10

> "And we know that for those who love God all things work together for good, for those who are called according to his purpose." **Romans 8:28**

"Relax! It Was Never About YOU Anyway!"

Year 10 begins, and my approach is very simple. The title says it all, ***Relax! It Was Never About You Anyway!*** God gave me an important assignment, challenges, tools, intelligence, support, and time to get it done. All the things I did and did not do as a Stepfather/StepDaddy were necessary and important for my Growth and Development and for the cohesion of the Blended Family Unit. I took lots of Ls because of **Me** and for **Me**. Now that **YOU** understand it was never about **YOU**. Accept the Challenge. Step Up! & Show Out! God is Watching!

StepDads Showing Up & Showing Out Final Tips

Tip 1: Check your feelings at the door, this is a hard, but rewarding work, if **YOU** stay in it, so expect and embrace those challenges. Don't be arrogant and naïve like me at the beginning. **Show Up & Show Out!**

Tip 2: Recognize that a family system was in place before you got there, so learn what that system is and be flexible and watchful in your approach to your spouse and children. **Show Up & Show Out!**

Tip 3: Check your *Love Languages, Multiple Intelligences, Unresolved Childhood and Adult Issues, Mental Health*, and evaluate your Spiritual Gifts before **YOU** begin this journey. If YOU are already in it, it's not too late to review your Blended Family Tools. **Show Up & Show Out!**

Tip 4: PRIDE is still before the Fall, so **YOU** know you are the MAN, they know you are the MAN, but that just means that **YOU** are Responsible! **Show Up & Show Out!**

Tip 5: Develop and interact and thank your "Wise Counsel" for helping you navigate challenges in your Blended Family. Learn from their experiences and accept their Wisdom. Do not be insecure like I was.

MEN with families are very good at counseling other MEN with families. **Show Up & Show Out!**

Tip 6: Recognize that your Wife and Mother of the Blended Family will always Love the Children more than **YOU**! That is by design and has nothing to do with **YOU**! **YOU** are striving for a different kind of LOVE! **Show Up & Show Out!**

Tip 7: Work to please God and watch the emotional, psychological, spiritual, and financial challenges **YOU** go through ease up. **Show Up & Show Out!**

Tip 8: Recognize that **YOU** <u>Will Be Changed</u> during this process. Misunderstandings will lead to Knowledge, Disagreements will lead to Discernment, Struggles will lead to Breakthroughs, and **YOU** will GROW! **Show Up & Show Out!**

Tip 9: Always Look Back, but then quickly Look Forward. **YOU** are not the same person **YOU** used to be, so always Move Forward! **Show Up & Show Out!**

Tip 10: This Blended Family Experience has never only been about **YOU**. God gave **YOU** as a MAN, an Important Assignment, and the tools to Get The Job Done!

Show Up! & Show Out!

YEAR CHAPTER REFERENCES

Year 1

1. Cerruti C. Building a functional multiple intelligences theory to advance educationalneuroscience. Front Psychol. 2013;4:950. doi:10.3389/fpsyg.2013.00950
2. Cherry, Kendra. "Erik Erikson's Stages of Psychosocial Development." *Verywell Mind*, Verywellmind, 10 Oct. 2005, www.verywellmind.com/erik-eriksons-stages-of-psychosocial-development-2795740.
3. "Coast to Coast AM." *Wikipedia*, 9 June 2020, en.wikipedia.org/wiki/Coast to Coast AM. Accessed 20 May 2020.
4. Evans, David G. *Dare to Be a Man : The Truth Every Man Must Know—and Every Woman Needs to Know about Him*. New York, Berkley ; London, 2010.
5. "Extract." *Dictionary.com*, Dictionary.com, www.dictionary.com/browse/extract. Accessed on May 15, 2020
6. Family Dynamics. "Advantages of Living in a Blended Family." *Secureteen.com*, accessed on December 8, 2018 from https://www.secureteen.com/blended-family/advantages-of-living-in-a-blended-family/

7. Ferrell, Will, et al. "Step Brothers." *IMDb*, 25 July 2008, www.imdb.com/title/tt0838283/.
8. Gardner H. *Frames of Mind: The Theory of Multiple Intelligences.* New York: Basic Books;1983.
9. Gillespie, Natalie N. "Blended Families." *Focus on the Family*, Focus on the Family, accessed on December 6, 2018, from https://www.focusonthefamily.com/lifechallenges/relationship-challenges/blended-families/blended-families
10. Scaccia, Annamarya. "How to Recognize and Treat the Symptoms of a Nervous Breakdown." *Healthline*, Healthline Media, 13 Aug. 2019, www.healthline.com/health/mental-health/nervous-breakdown.
11. "Soul Train." *Wikipedia*, 29 May 2020, en.wikipedia.org/wiki/Soul Train. Accessed 15 May 2020.
12. Sternberg RJ. Intelligence. *Dialogues Clin Neurosci.* 2012;14(1):19-27.
13. "Types of Intelligence and How to Find The One You Are Best In." *Cleverism*, 2 June 2017, www.cleverism.com/types-of-intelligence/.
14. "Wabbaseka, Arkansas." *Wikipedia*, 10 Apr. 2020, en.wikipedia.org/wiki/Wabbaseka. Accessed 15 May 2020.

Year 2

1. Evans, David G. *Dare to Be a Man : The Truth Every Man Must Know—and Every Woman Needs to Know about Him.* New York, Berkley ; London, 2010.

2. Mcleod, Saul. "Maslow's Hierarchy of Needs." *Simply Psychology*, 20 Mar. 2020, www.simplypsychology.org/maslow.html#:~:text=Maslow.
3. Papernow, P. L. (2013). *Surviving and thriving in stepfamily relationships: What works and what doesn't*. Routledge/Taylor & Francis Group.

Year 3

1. Chapman, Gary D. *The 5 Love Languages*. Chicago, Northfield Pub, 2015.
2. Rice, S. C. (2010). *Four tubas, a guitar, and a gallery of cheerleaders : Transition in the life of a Black Ph.D. ; a first person narrative*. Bloomington, Ind.: Authorhouse.

Year 4

1. How to Use Cut off your nose to spite your face Correctly – Grammarist. (n.d.). Retrieved May 10, 2020, from grammarist.com website: https://grammarist.com/usage/cut-off-your-nose-to-spite-your-face/
2. Today's Military. "Boot Camp." https://www.todaysmilitary.com/joining-eligibility/boot-camp 15 May. 2020. Accessed 20 May 2020.
3. West Midland Family Center. (n.d.). Retrieved June 16, 2020, from wmfc.org website: http://wmfc.org/about/publications.html

Year 5

1. "History of Military Cadences." *Military Cadence*, 5 Oct. 2014, www.army-cadence.com/history-of-miltary-cadences/.
2. Marlatt, Greta E. "Research Guides: Military Music: Military Cadences & Chants." *Libguides.Nps.Edu*, libguides.nps.edu/militarymusic/cadences. Accessed 16 June 2020.

Year 6

1. Goyer, David S, et al. "Man of Steel." *IMDb*, 12 June 2013, www.imdb.com/title/tt0770828/.
2. "Importance of Effective Communication." *Professional Development for Leaders and Managers of Self-Governing Schools*, pp. 197–215, ysrinfo.files.wordpress.com/2012/06/effectivecommunication5.pdf.
3. Melinda. (2019). HelpGuide.org. Retrieved from HelpGuide.org website: https://www.helpguide.org/articles/relationships-communication/nonverbal-communication.htm
4. "Stop Keeping Score: Busting the Myth That the Division of Labor in a Relationship Should Be 50/50." *Kate Hanley*, 8 Aug. 2018, katehanley.com/stop-keeping-score-busting-the-myth-that-the-division-of-labor-in-a-relationship-should-be-50-50/. Accessed 15 May 2020.
5. "These Are the 7 Types of Love." *Psychology Today*, 2016, www.psychologytoday.com/us/blog/hide-and-seek/201606/these-are-the-7-types-love.

Year 7

1. Evans, David G. *Dare to Be a Man : The Truth Every Man Must Know—and Every Woman Needs to Know about Him.* New York, Berkley ; London, 2010.

Year 8

1. Robertson, Arnold E. *God's Planned Parenthood.* 2016.
2. "Spiritual Gifts | FREE Spiritual Gifts Survey | Assessment, Analysis, Test." *Spiritual Gifts Survey*, 2018, gifts.churchgrowth.org/spiritual-gifts-survey/.
3. *Your Spiritual Gifts – How to Identify and Effectively Use Them. – Unfolding Faith Blog.* www.tyndale.com/sites/unfoldingfaithblog/2018/11/13/your-spiritual-gifts-how-to-identify-and-effectively-use-them/. Accessed 15 May 2020.

Please note that none of my formal educational training, prepared me to be somebody's **STEPFATHER (STEPDAD)**. This is one of the most important points of the book and of my life. I thought I was ready and truly believed I had the education, experience, training, and financial means to be the greatest STEPFATHER (STEPDAD) I knew.

Truth is, I did not know Jack! It took me years to understand what I <u>did not</u> know and that I was not smart enough to do this Blended Family work on my own. I had to trust God, recognize my assignment, seek advice, work hard, take LLs, be patient, and learn by doing!!!

(Photo used with permission from Troy Baker Photography)

> Your Challenge!
>
> Always
>
> Show Up & Show Out!
>
> God Bless!

STEPDADDY/DADDY PHOTO ALBUM

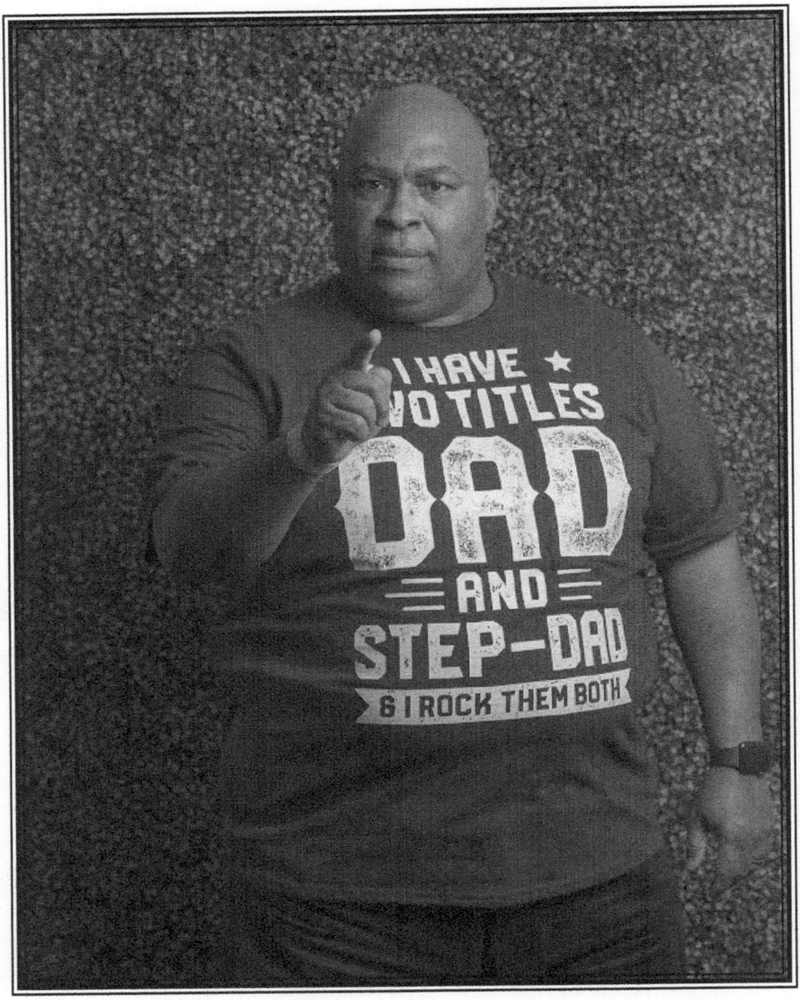
I HAVE
WO TITLES
DAD
AND
STEP-DAD
& I ROCK THEM BOTH

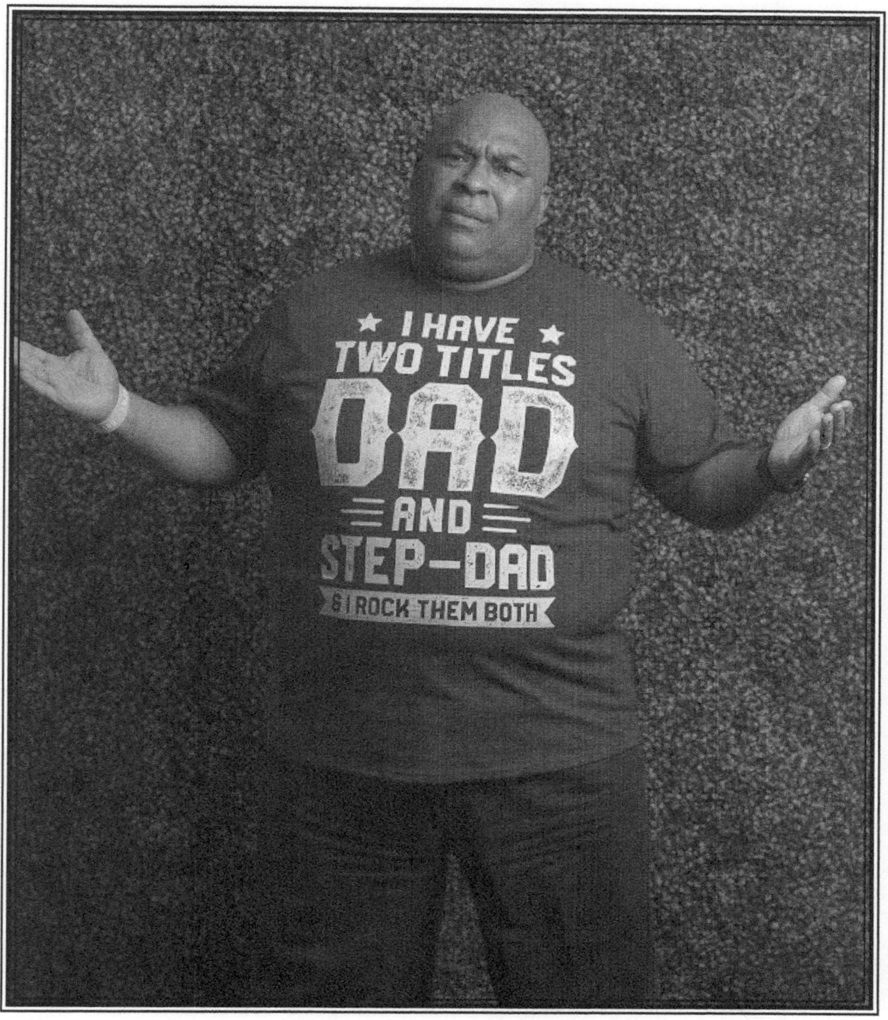
I HAVE
TWO TITLES
DAD
AND
STEP-DAD
& I ROCK THEM BOTH

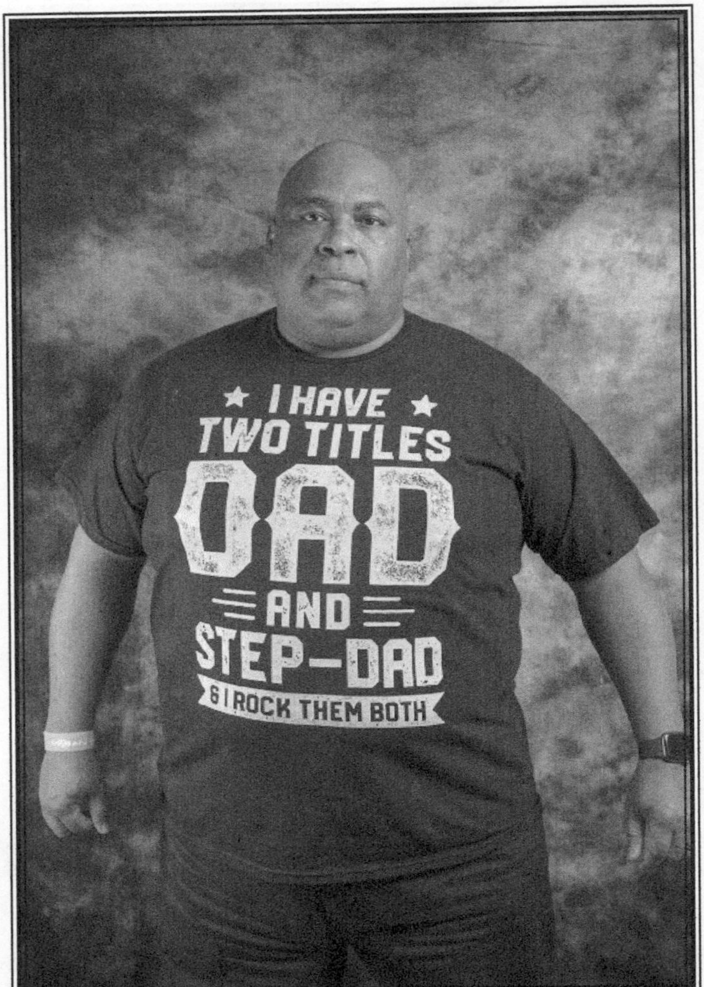
I HAVE
TWO TITLES
DAD
AND
STEP-DAD
& I ROCK THEM BOTH

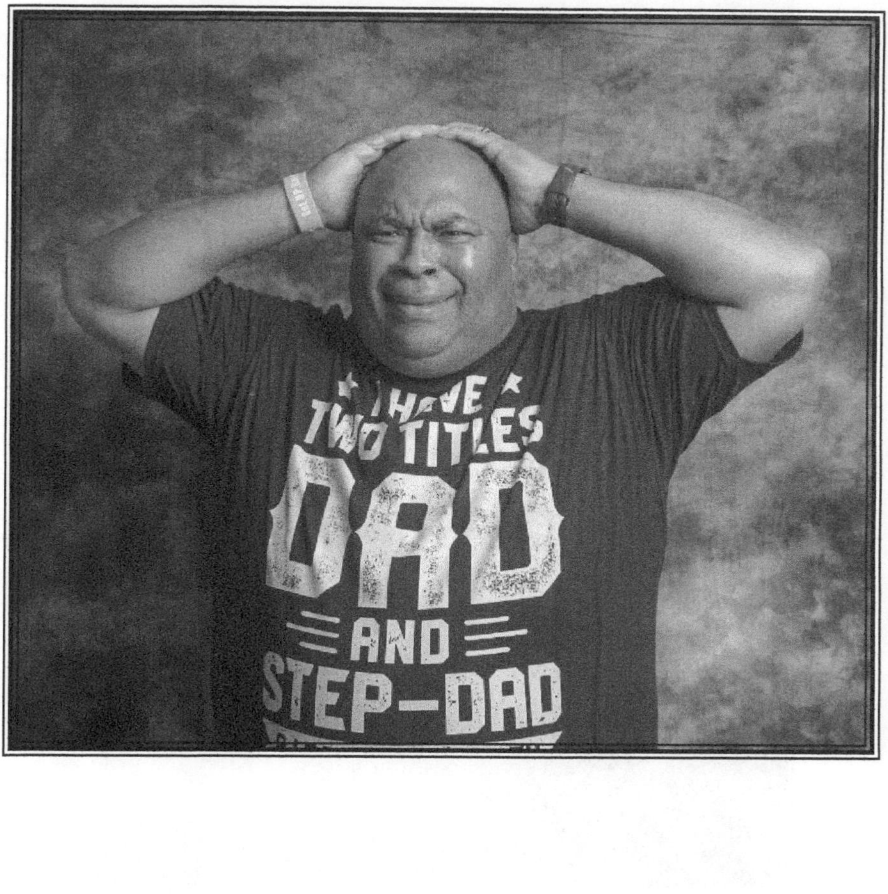
TWO TITLES
DAD
AND
STEP-DAD

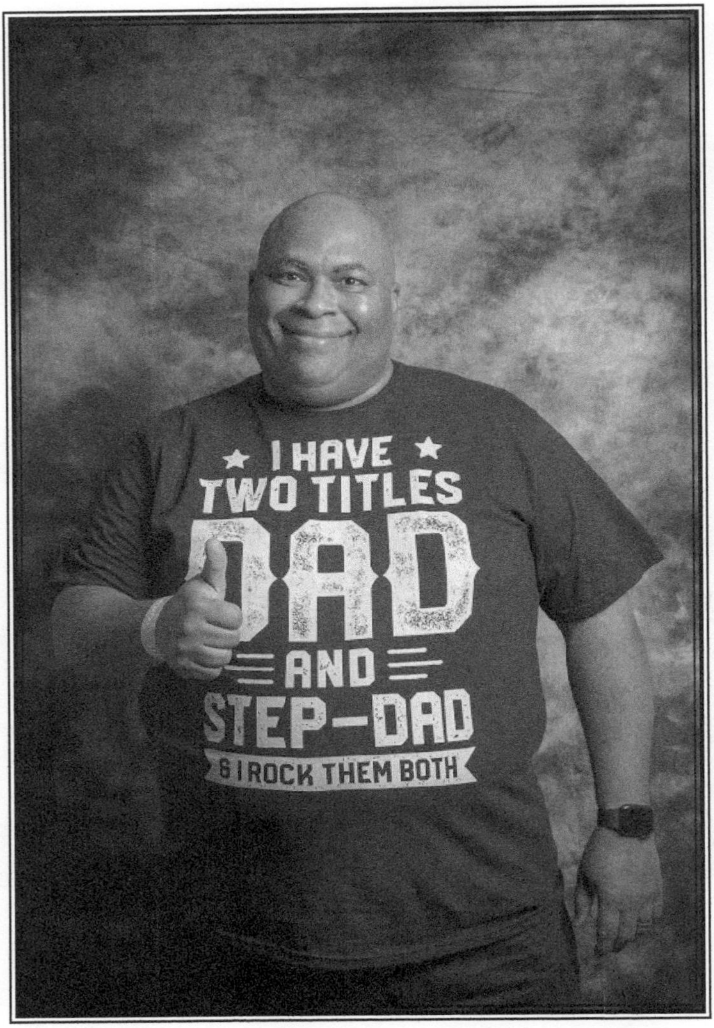
I HAVE
TWO TITLES
DAD
AND
STEP-DAD
& I ROCK THEM BOTH

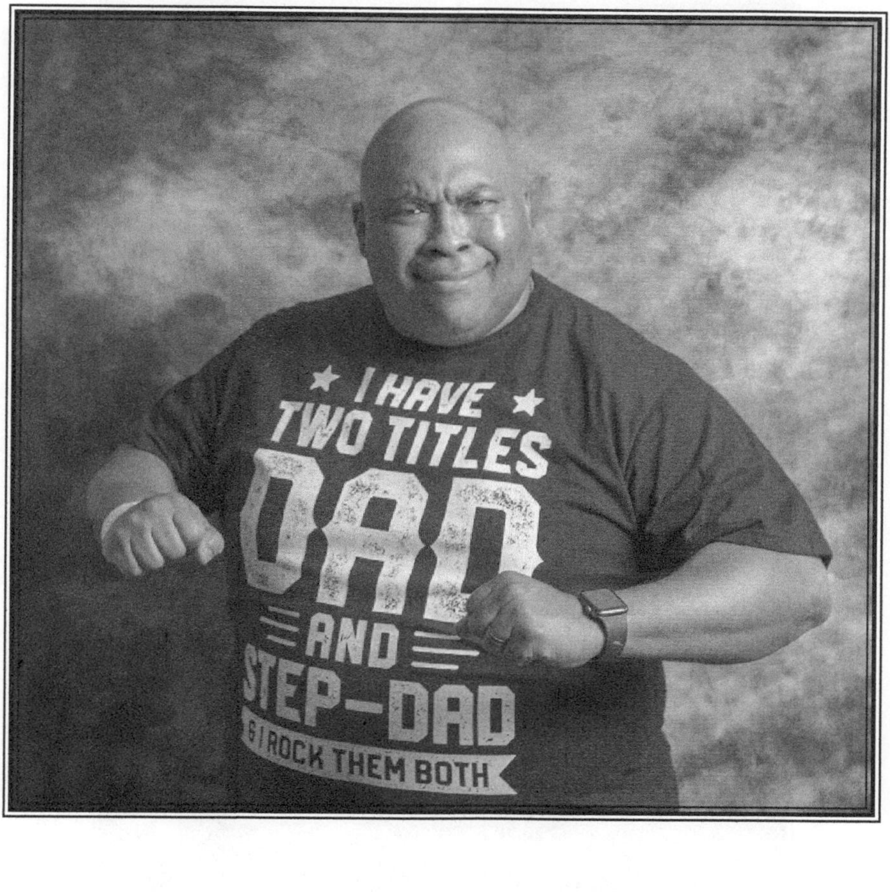
I HAVE
TWO TITLES
DAD
AND
STEP-DAD
& I ROCK THEM BOTH

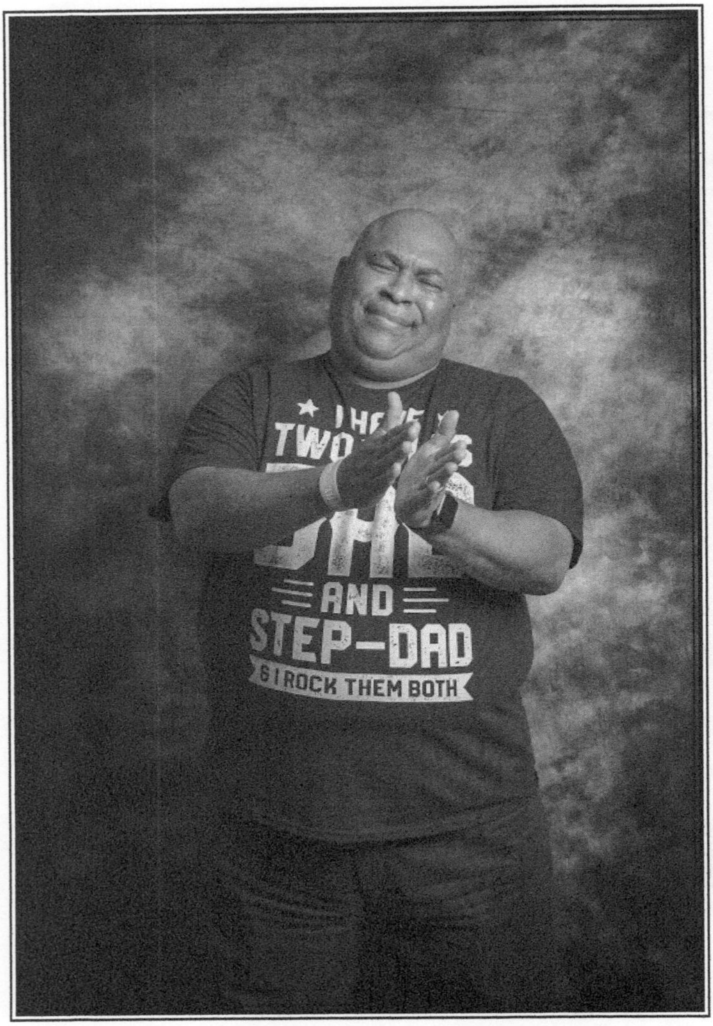
AND
STEP-DAD
& I ROCK THEM BOTH

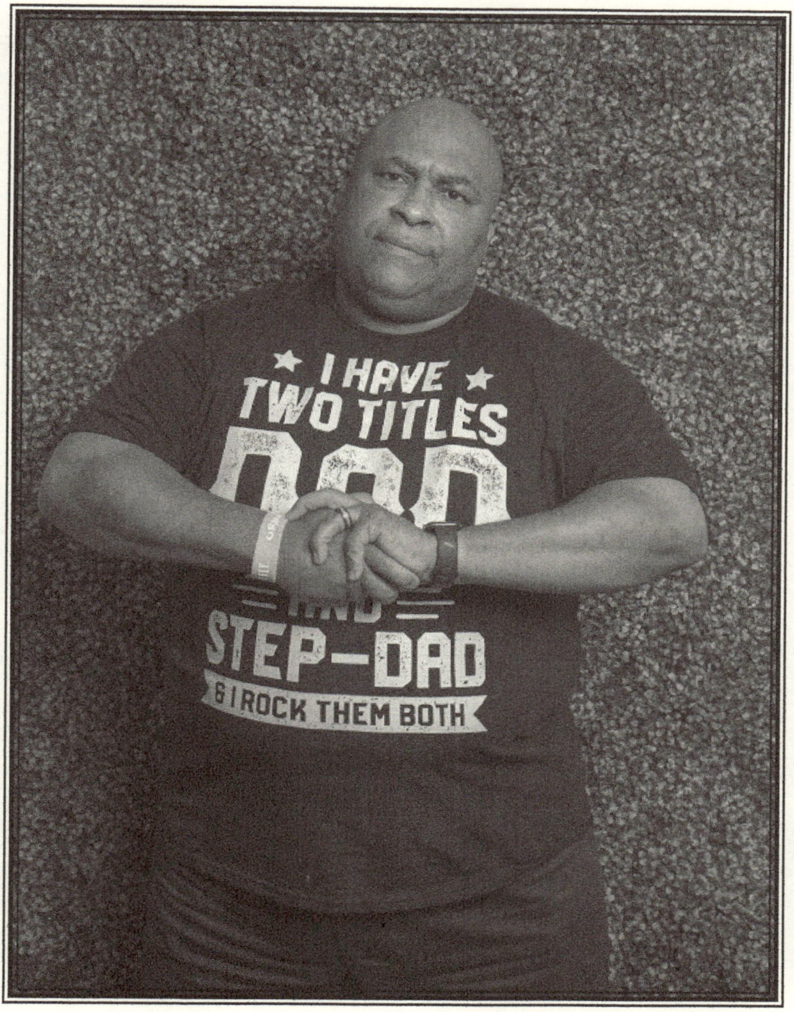
I HAVE
TWO TITLES
STEP-DAD
& I ROCK THEM BOTH

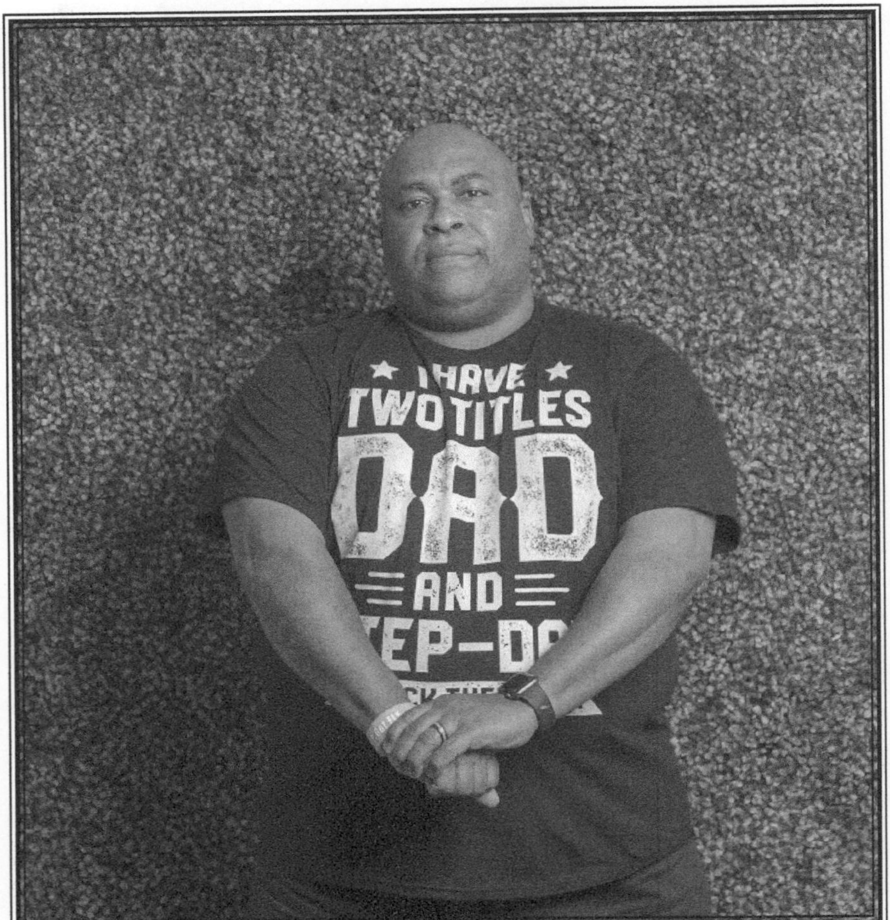
I HAVE
TWO TITLES
DAD
AND

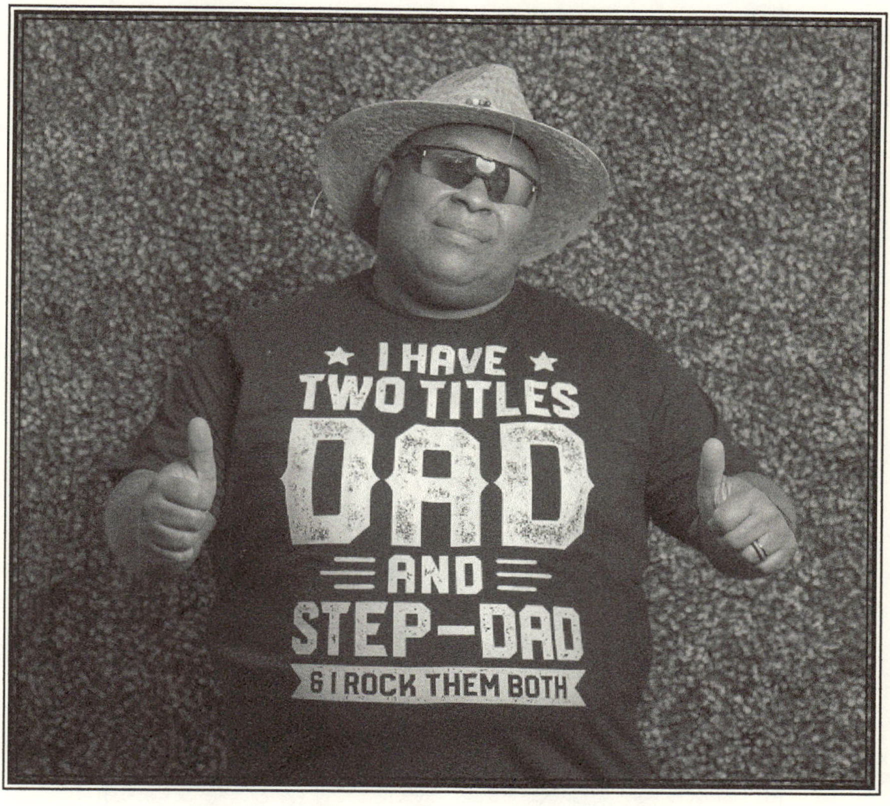
I HAVE
TWO TITLES
DAD
AND
STEP-DAD
& I ROCK THEM BOTH

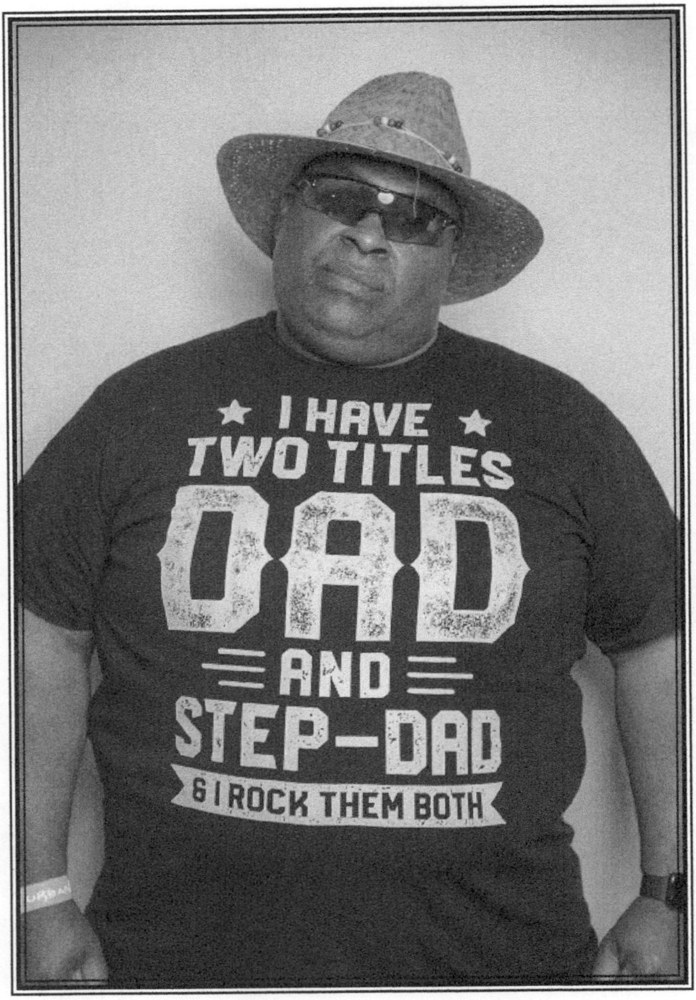
I HAVE
TWO TITLES
DAD
AND
STEP-DAD
& I ROCK THEM BOTH

God is Good!

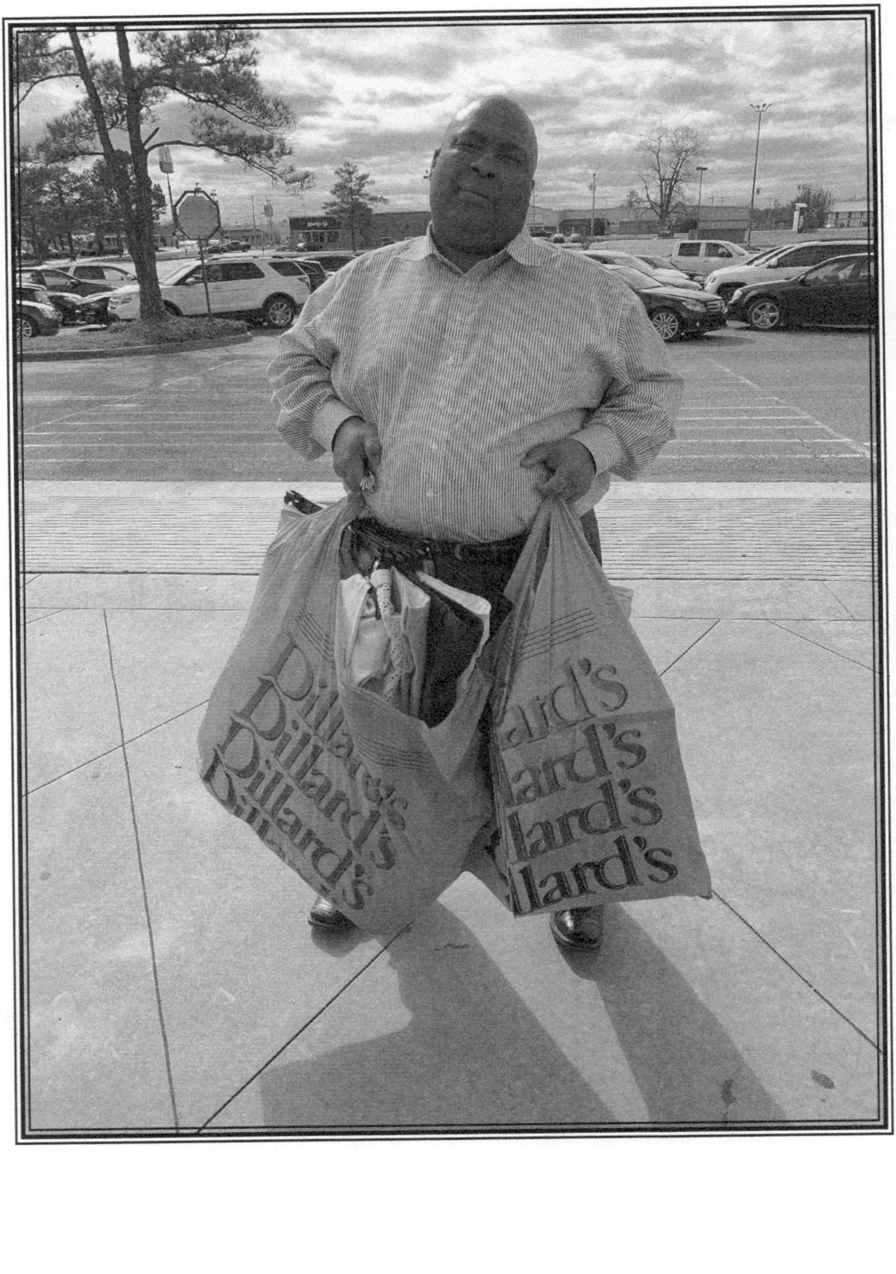
Dillard's

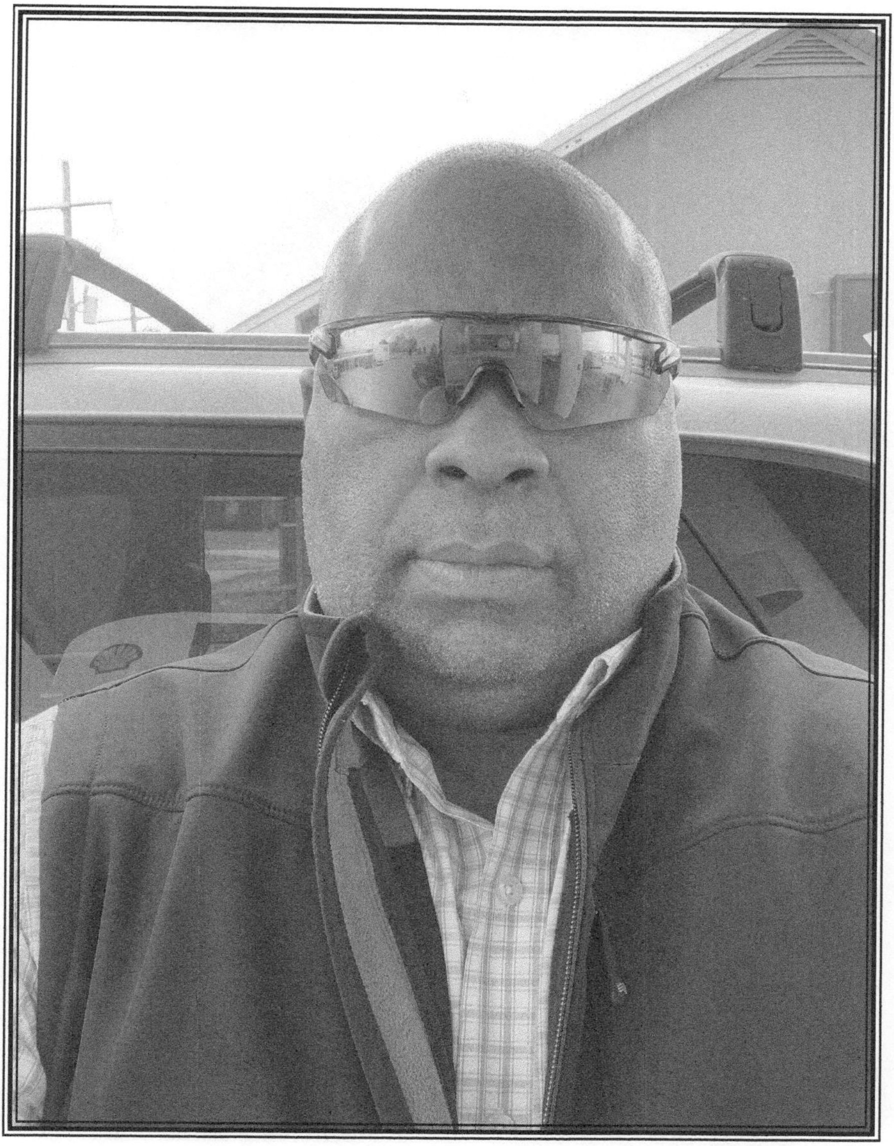

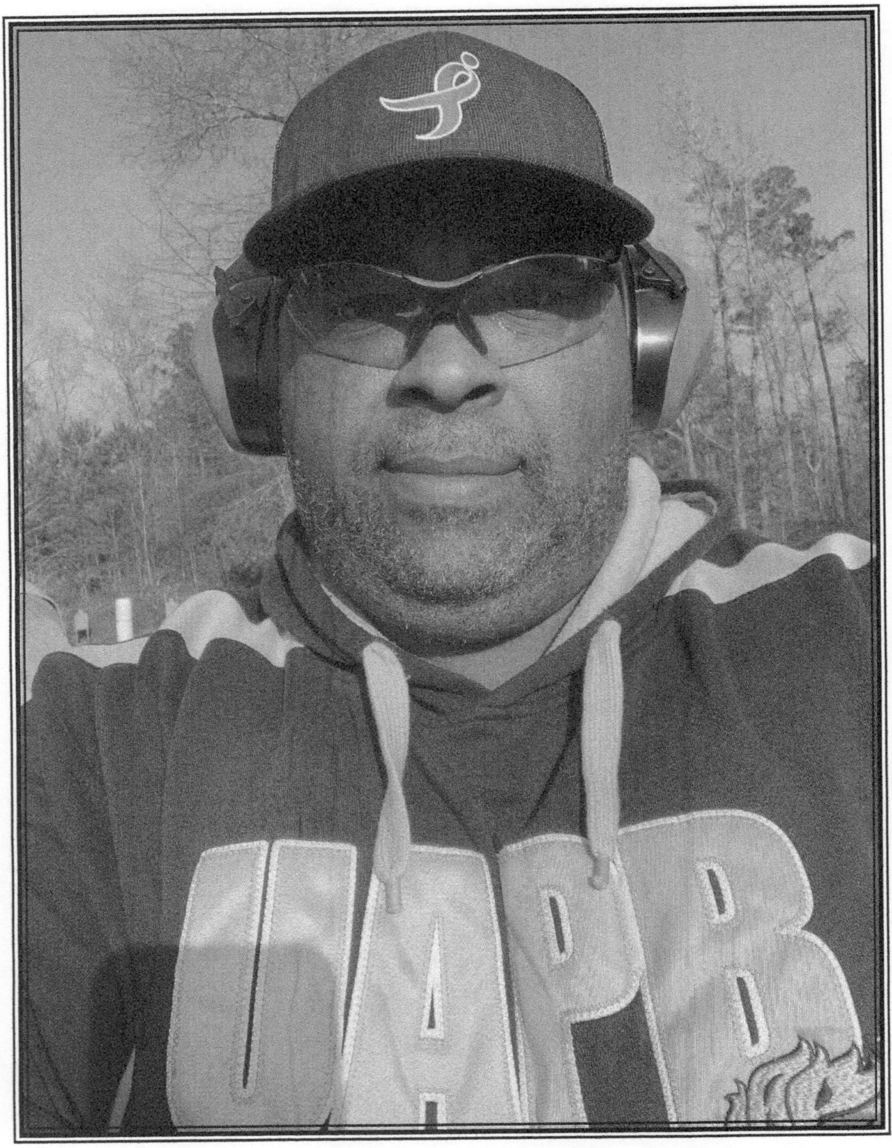
UAPB

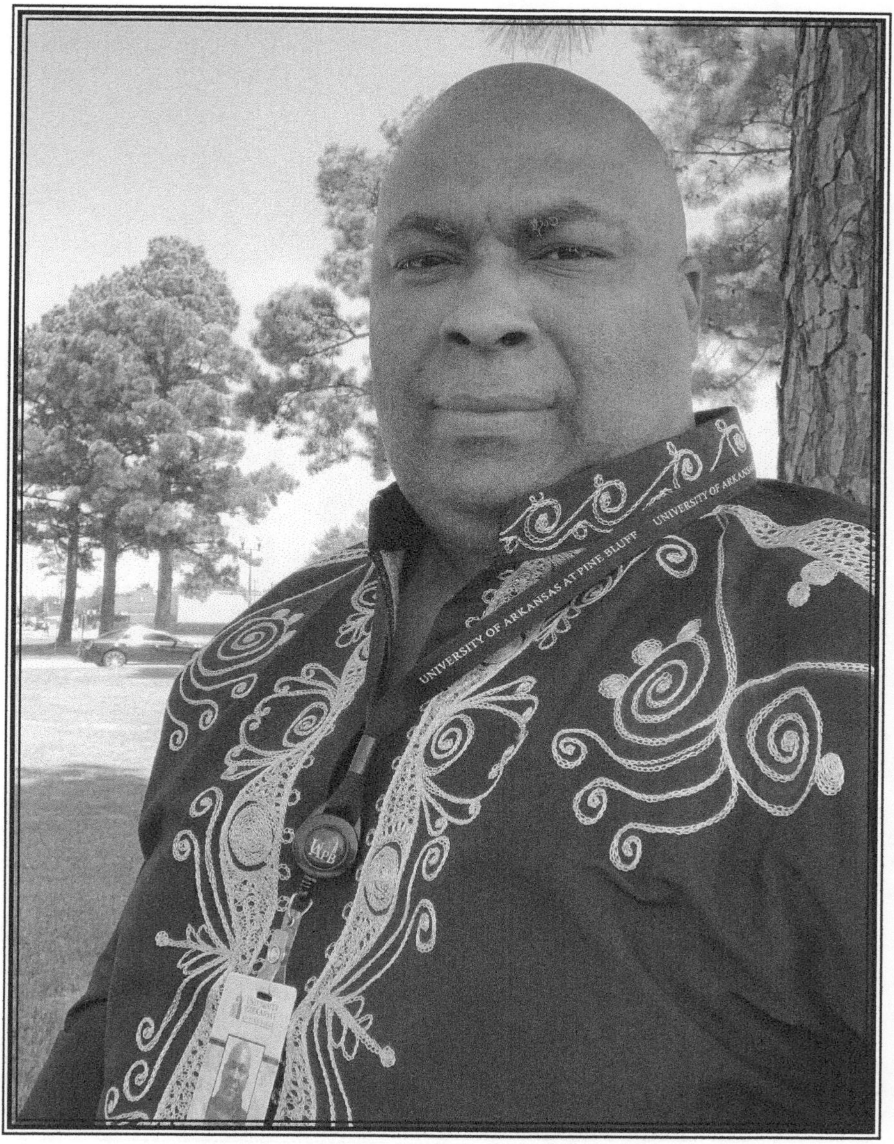
UNIVERSITY OF ARKANSAS AT PINE BLUFF

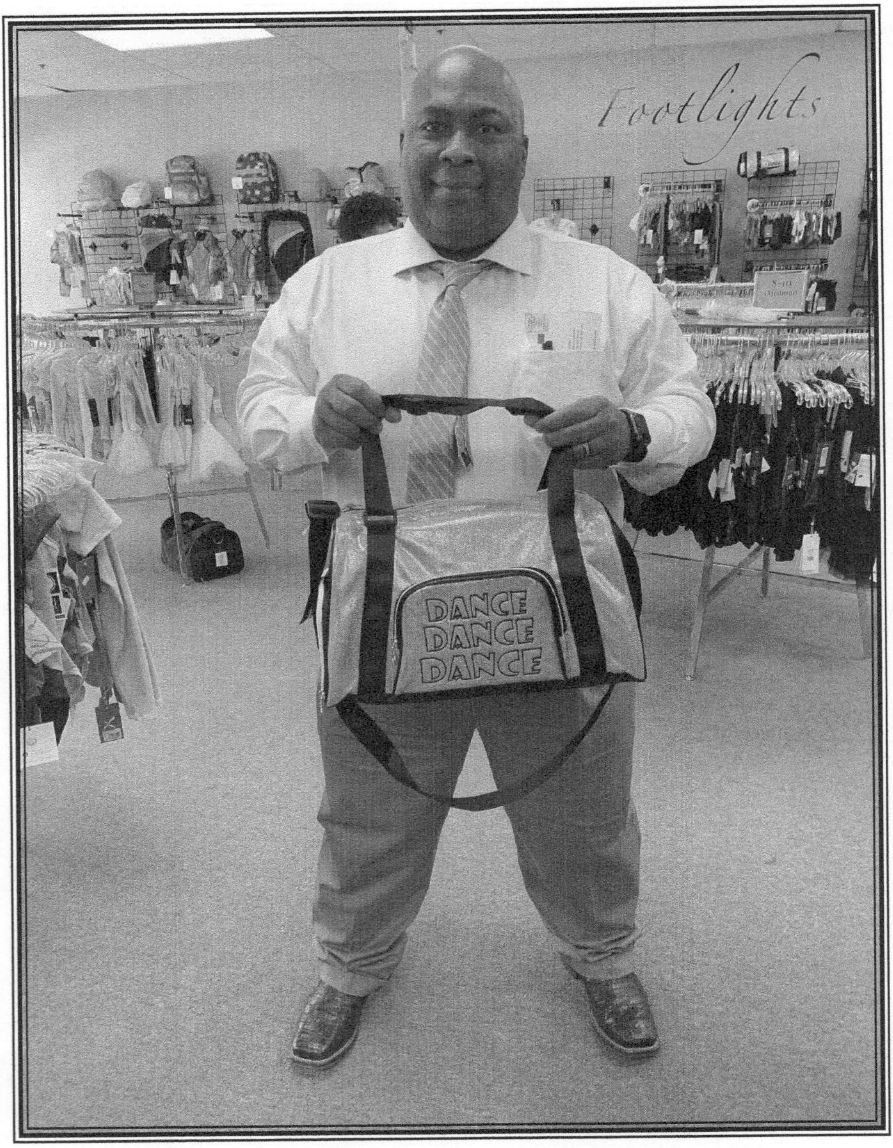
Footlights
DANCE
DANCE
DANCE

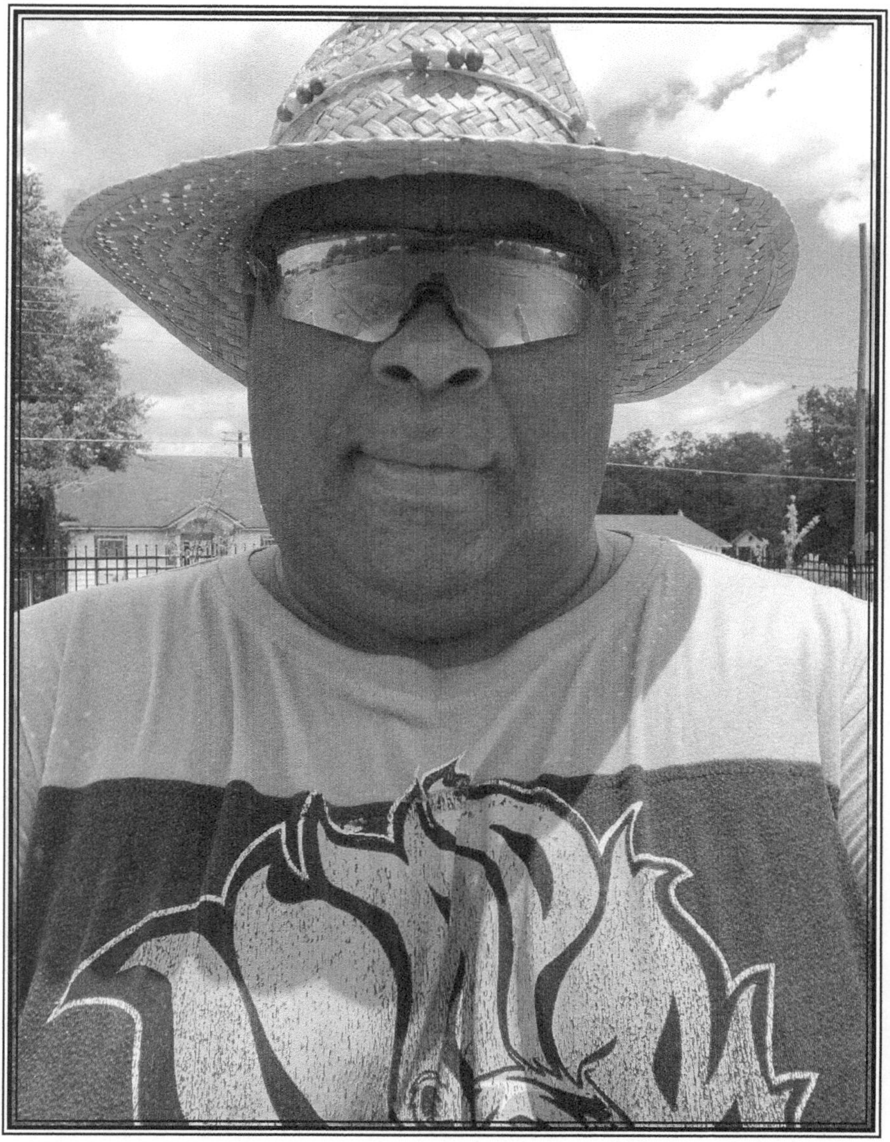

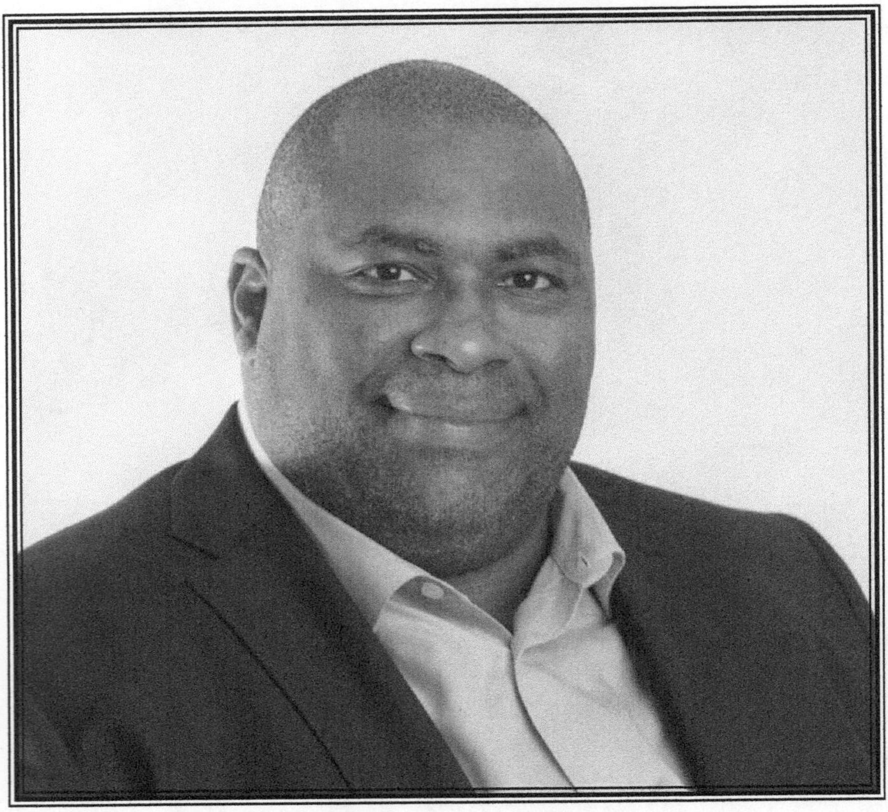

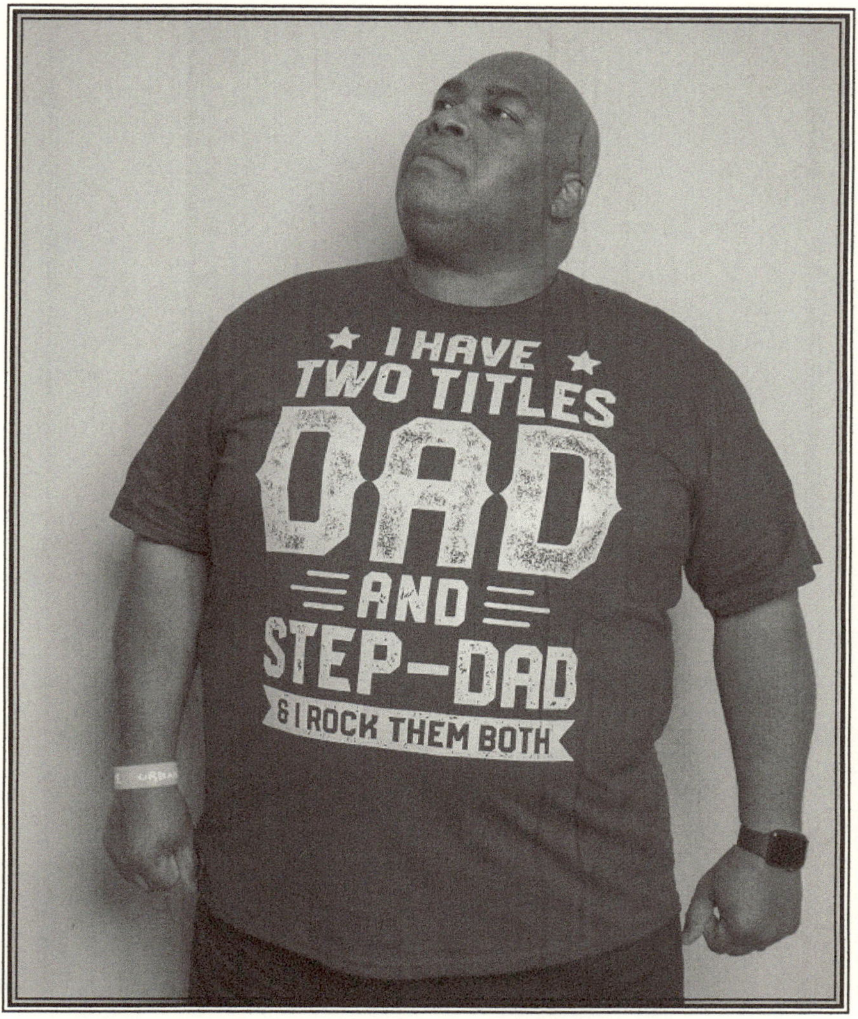
I HAVE
TWO TITLES
DAD
AND
STEP-DAD
& I ROCK THEM BOTH

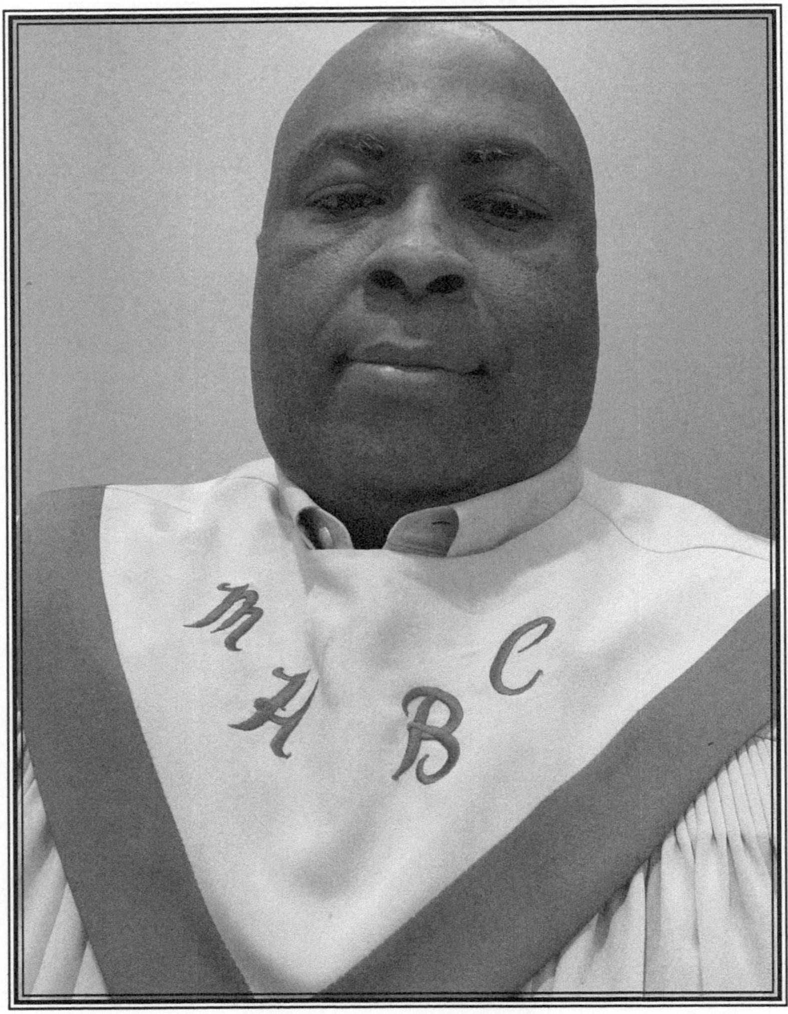
M
A
B
C

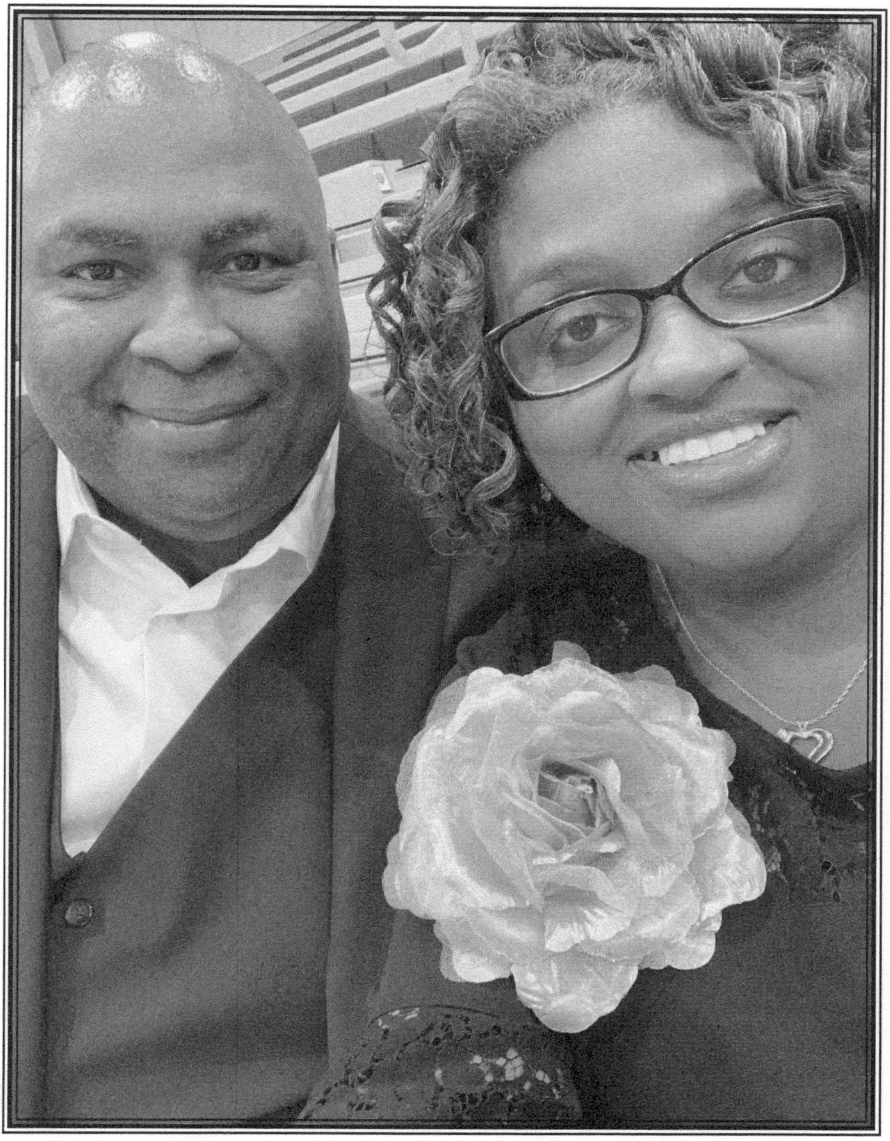

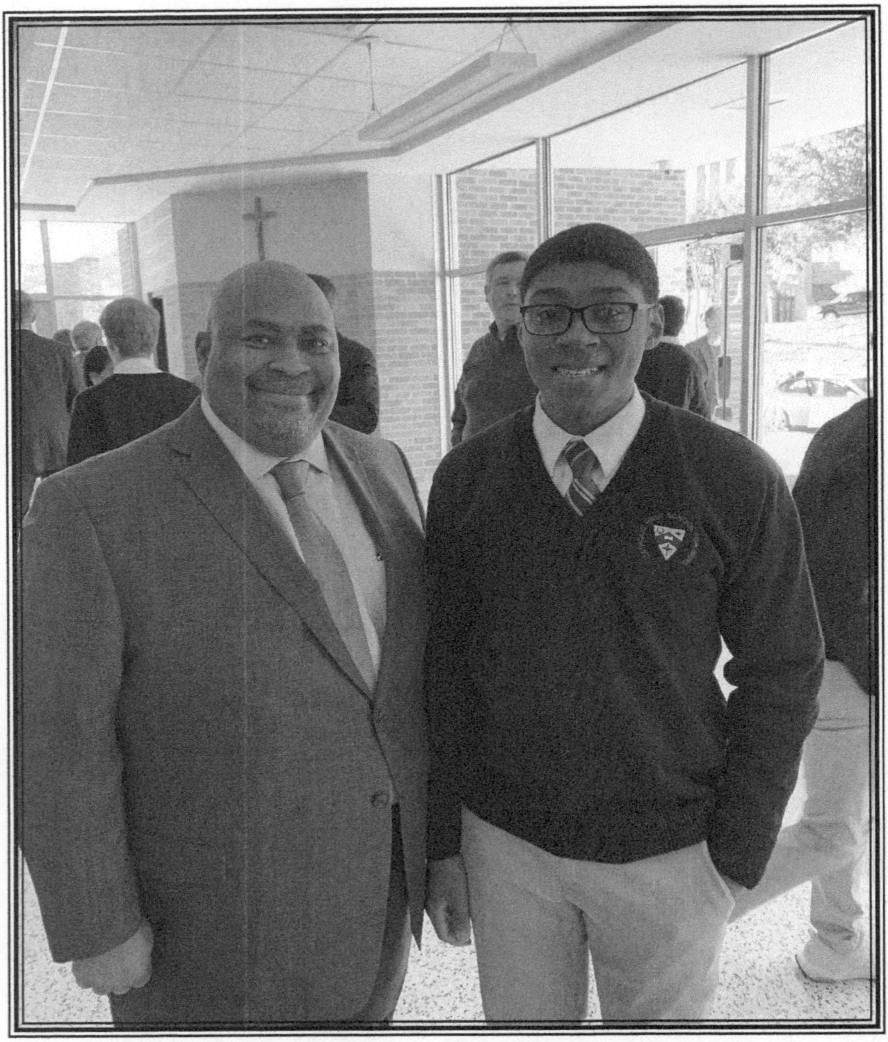

ARKANSAS
STATE POLICE
MAIN ENTRANCE
DIRECTOR'S OFFICE
ADMINISTRATIVE SERVICES DIVISION
CRIMINAL INVESTIGATION DIVISION
HIGHWAY PATROL DIVISION
REGULATORY DIVISION
•CRASH RECORDS
•STATE FIRE MARSHAL
•CONCEALED HANDGUN CAR
•PI/SECURITY/ALARM COMPA
•USED MOTOR VEHICLE DEAL
CRIMES AGAINST CHILDREN
COMMISSION ON LAW EN
STANDARDS AND TRAINING
WEST ENTRANCE

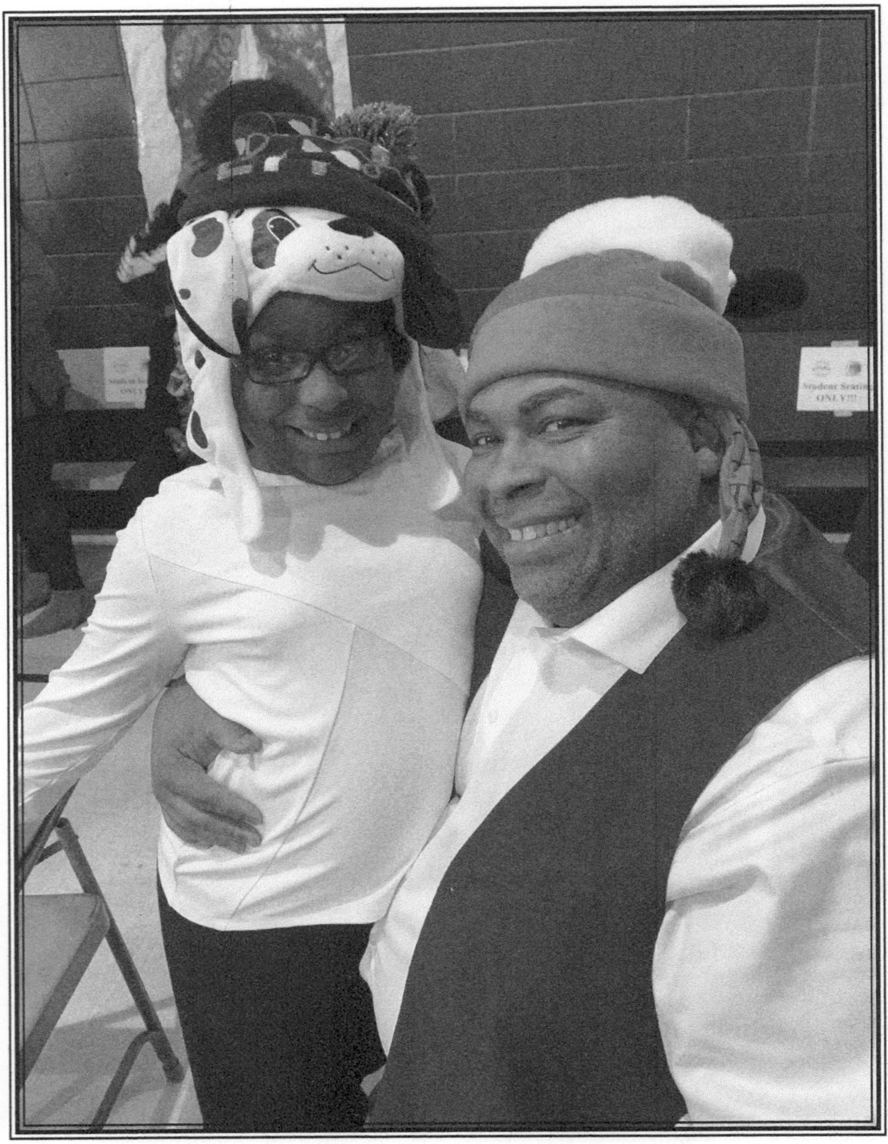

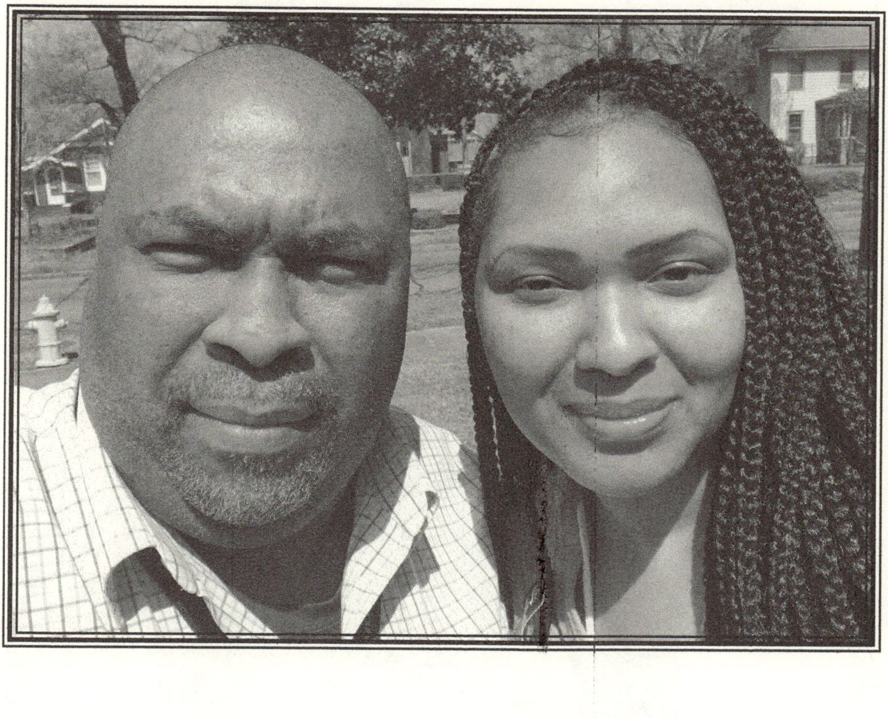

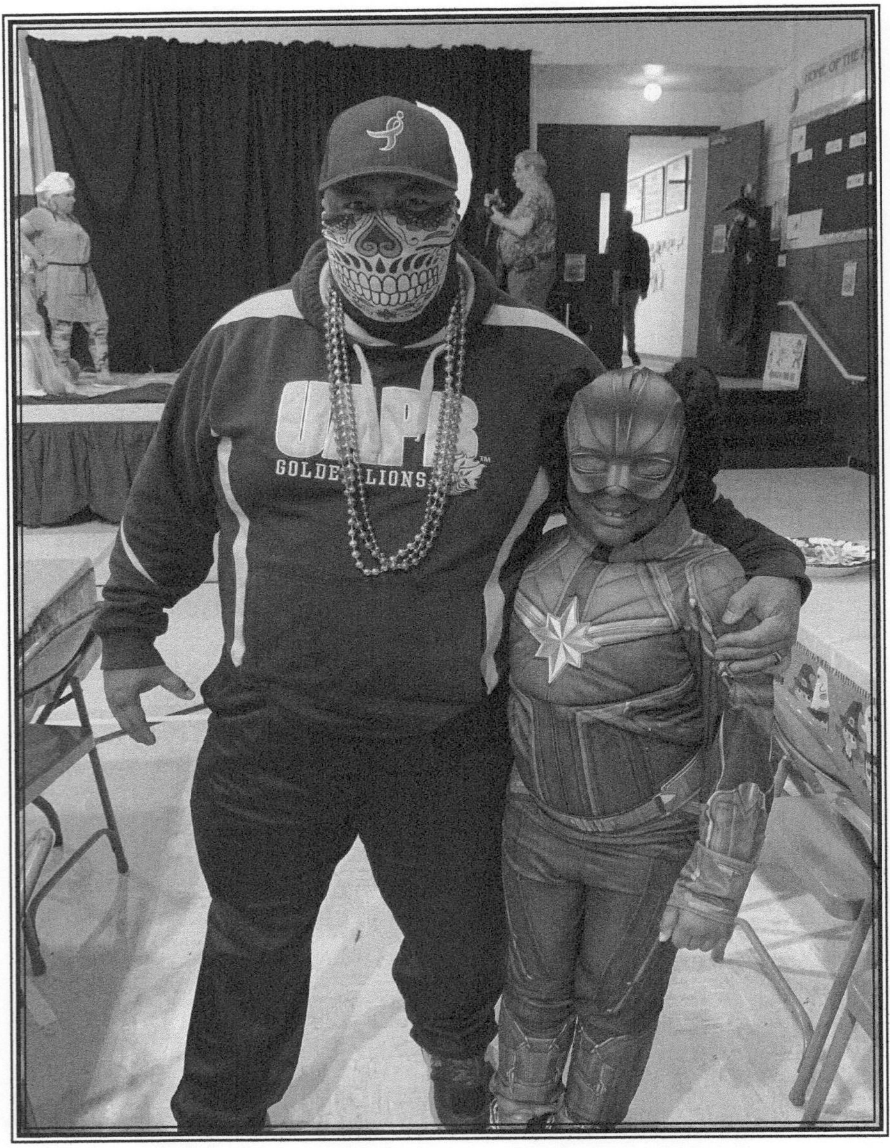
UAPB
LIONS

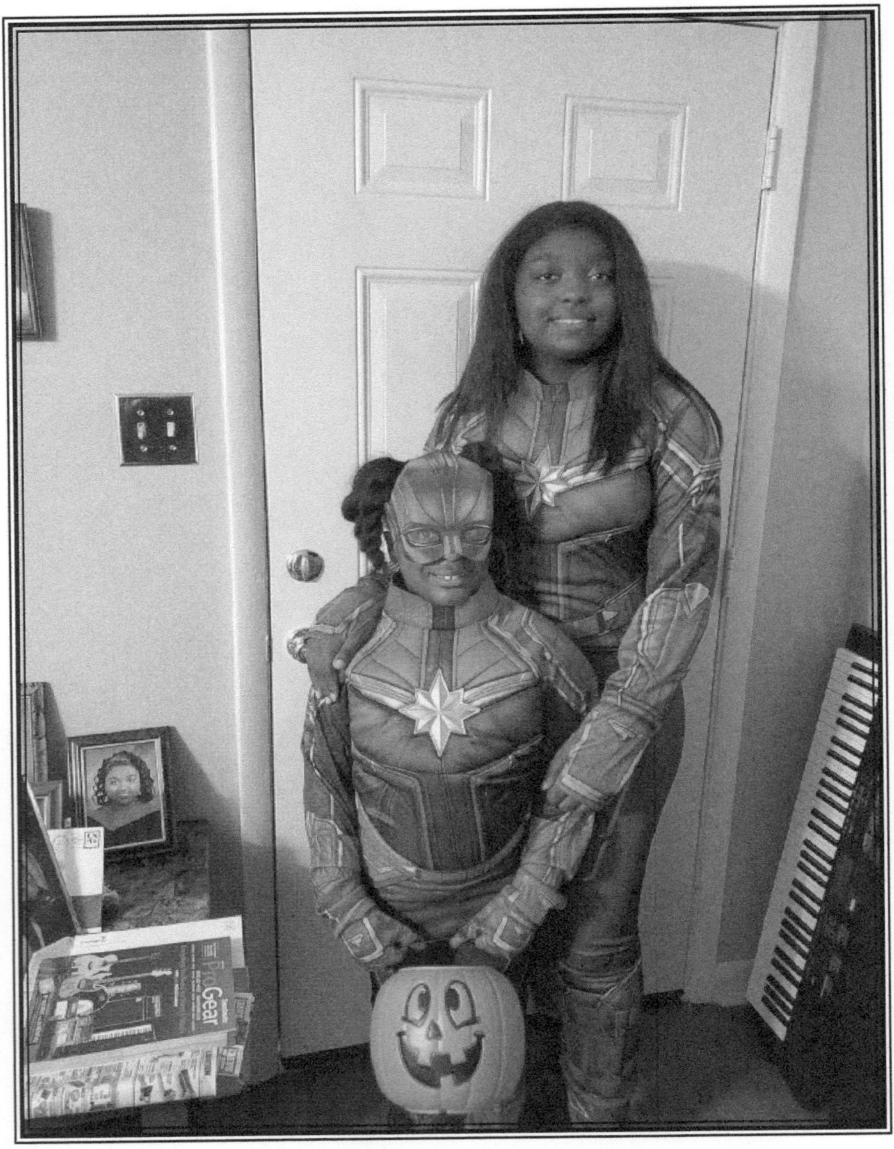
ProGear

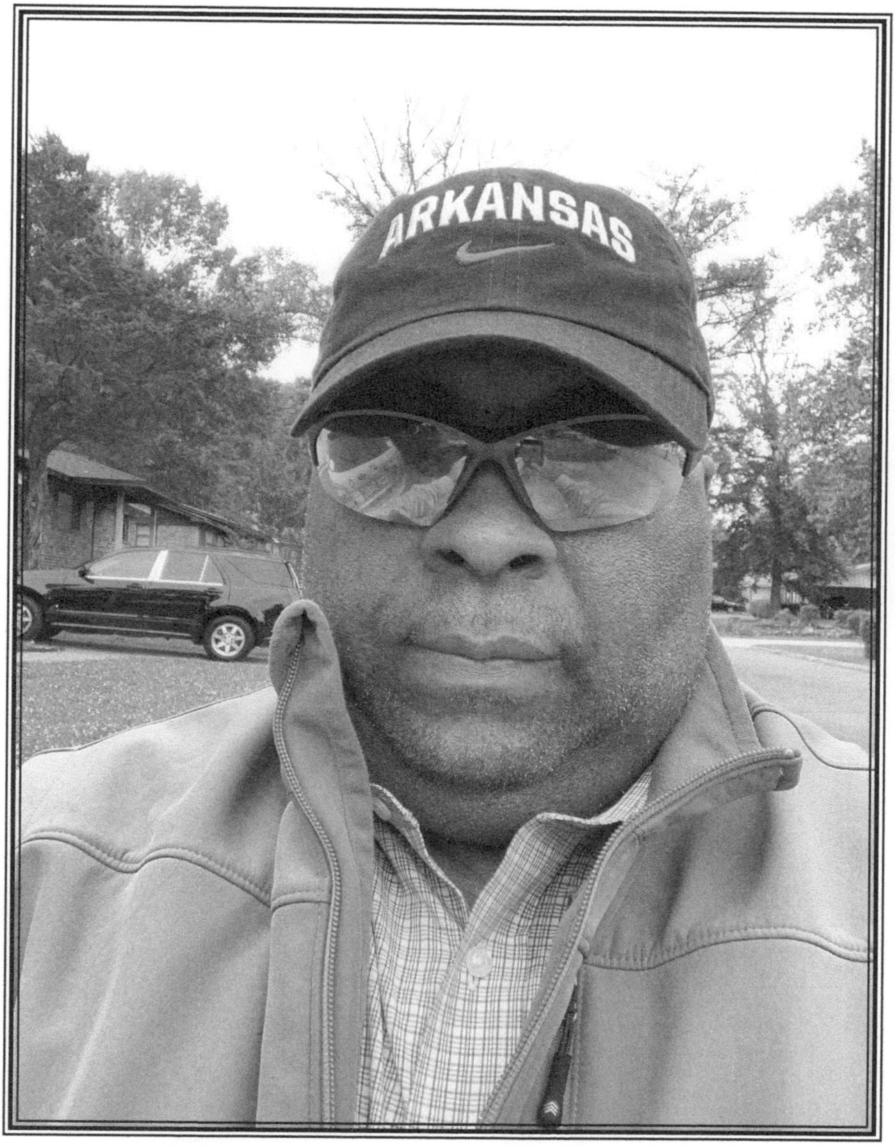
ARKANSAS

FOREWORD AUTHOR

Josiah J. Sampson, III, Ph.D.

Josiah J. Sampson, III, Ph.D. Biography

Dr. Josiah J. Sampson, III is a native of Jackson, Mississippi. He holds the following degrees; Bachelor of Science in Biology from Jackson State University, Bachelor of Arts in Sociology from Elizabeth City State University, Master of Education from Tennessee State University, and a Doctor of Philosophy from Meharry Medical College. He has also been a CASL Fellow and has done advanced studies in Public Administration at the University of Alabama. Dr. Sampson has served in education at multiple levels for over twenty years. He has also served in multiple capacities in faith-based communities and others social and civic arenas. His academic and nonacademic service record has caused him to be a highly sought, reliable resource when called upon. Dr. Sampson has published articles in peer-review journals and has done a plethora of interviews and writings on various subjects.

PROOFREADER/EDITOR

Miss Willingham

Miss Willingham's Biography

Miss Willingham is a native of Stephens, Arkansas. She attended the public schools of Stephens. Upon graduation, she attended the Agricultural Mechanical & Normal (AM&N) College in Pine Bluff, Arkansas, where she received a Bachelor of Science Degree in Business Education. She began her career as a Business Education teacher at her High School Alma Mater, Carver High School, and taught one year (1968-69). She then received a job offer from the newly organized ROTC Department at AM&N. She accepted the job as secretary, with excitement and returned to her Alma Mater. She served in that position for 5 years and subsequently, accepted another position at the School as Assistant to the Acting Chancellor, Dr. J. B. Johnson.

In 1977, Miss Willingham relocated to Atlanta, Georgia and served in several positions over time. She enjoyed a 22-Year (1985-2007) work experience as Program Officer in the Office of International Health Programs at Morehouse School of Medicine, before moving to Durham, North Carolina. She was then employed at North Carolina Central University (NCCU), Durham, North Carolina, as Assistant to the Chancellor and served in that position for seven years

(2007-2014) before being promoted to the position of Ombudsperson. She served in that position until retirement in 2016.

Miss Willingham now resides in her hometown of Stephens, Arkansas, where she serves her church, New Home A.M.E. Church, as a Steward, Director of Christian Education, and Adult Sunday School Teacher. She is also a member of the Alpha Kappa Alpha Sorority, Inc., and a member of the AM&N/UAPB Alumni Association, Camden, Arkansas.

Fathers & Sons Clothier

Thank you for proudly serving our community for over 23 years, and for supporting this project.

S&S Publishing and Consulting, LLC

AUTHOR BIOGRAPHY

Dr. Sederick Charles Rice is a 1994 graduate of the University of Arkansas at Pine Bluff (UAPB), where he earned a Bachelor of Science degree in Biology, a 1996 graduate of Delaware State University, where he earned a Master of Science in Biology, and a 2003 graduate of the University of Vermont where he earned a Ph.D. in Cell & Molecular Biology. Following his doctoral studies, he worked for the National Center for Environmental Assessment (NCEA) in Washington, D.C., a division of the Environmental Protection Agency (EPA), as research scientist to study human health and risk assessment of chemical alloy pollutants in the environment. He is currently an associate professor of biology (tenured) and the former director (2016-2018) of the Math and Science Pre-College STEM Center at UAPB.

His current research adds to the body of knowledge on how educators translate data into visual displays, analyze and present statistical data, and identify instructor and students' strengths and weaknesses for using and benefiting from immersive 3D Immersive Virtual Reality (IVR) approaches across STEM interdisciplinary fields. Dr. Rice has conducted formative and summative assessments, using innovative technology, for more than ten years. He has collected and analyzed demographic data, with a focus on student learning and retention outcomes, within K-12, adult education learning, STEM undergraduate and graduate student populations, as well as in professional workplace environments. Dr. Rice is a board member of the Go Forward Pine Bluff Initiative, board member and vice-chair of the Arkansas Coordinated Child Effort in State Services (ACCESS, INC), Site Director for the HBCU-Med-Track Program (UAPB), Commissioner on the Pine Bluff Wastewater Commission, chair of the Arkansas Minority Health Commission, and is an active member of the UAPB/AM&N National Alumni Association.

Dr. Rice is married with children and is an active member and Deacon of his church. His keys to success are a strong relationship and belief in the power of God's Grace, Favor, and Mercy, mentor-relationships, laughter at all costs, support from family and friends, and a belief that Persistence, Hard work, and Dedication always leads to success.

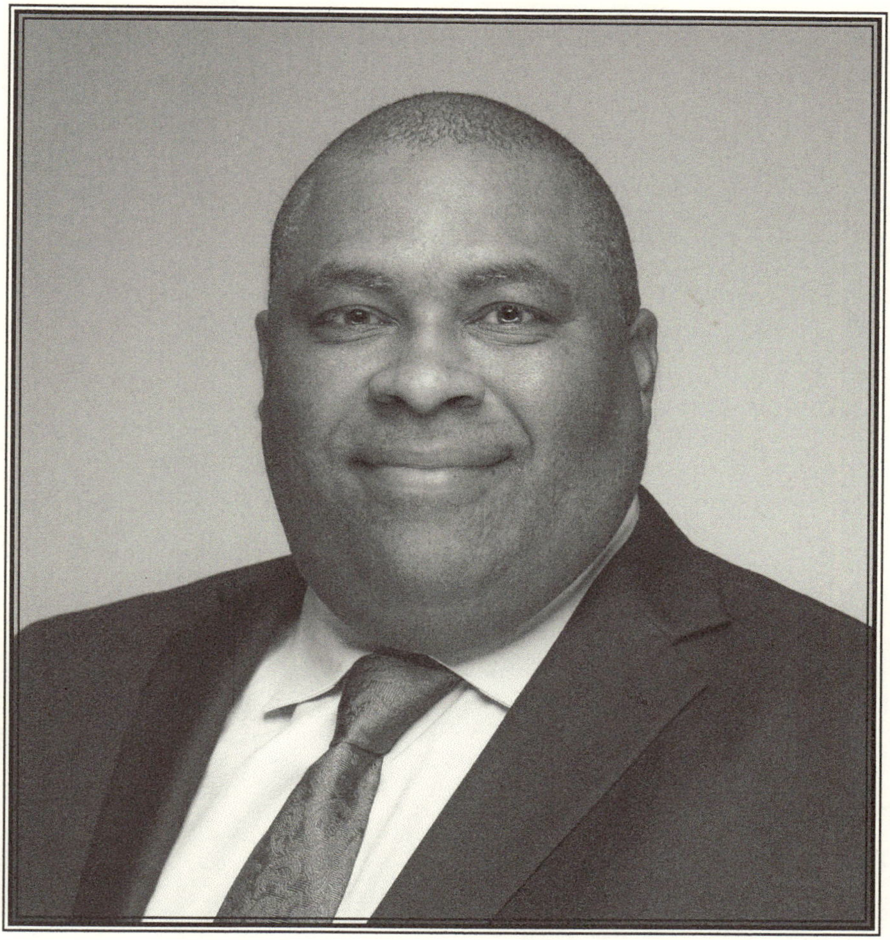